STEP STUDY COUNSELING WITH THE DUAL DISORDERED CLIENT

About the authors:

Katie Evans, CADC, is president of Evans and Sullivan, Inc., where she does counseling and consultation in Portland, Oregon. She is a certified alcohol and drug counselor. She has worked as a counselor, program director, and consultant in the area of dual diagnosis since 1984. She gives seminars and workshops throughout the United States on the topic of dual disorders and treatment of resistant adolescents.

J. Michael Sullivan, Ph.D., is an author, consultant, and clinician specializing in the areas of dual diagnosis, borderline personality disorder, and difficult-to-treat patients. He also gives workshops on the topic of mental health agencies. A clinical psychologist, Sullivan is clinical director of Evans and Sullivan, Inc., in Portland. He is also an assistant professor at the School of Professional Psychology, Pacific University, Forest Grove, Oregon.

STEP STUDY COUNSELING WITH THE DUAL DISORDERED CLIENT

KATIE EVANS & J. MICHAEL SULLIVAN

HAZELDEN®

First published October 1990.

ISBN: 0-89486-716-4
Library of Congress Catalog Card Number: 90-82292
Printed in the United States of America.

Editor's note:

Hazelden Educational Materials offers a variety of information on chemical dependency and related areas. Our publications do not necessarily represent Hazelden or its programs, nor do they officially speak for any Twelve Step organization.

Permission to reprint the Twelve Steps does not mean that Alcoholics Anonymous has reviewed or approved the contents of this publication, nor that AA agrees with the views expressed herein. AA is a program of recovery from alcoholism only. Use of the Twelve Steps in connection with programs which are patterned after AA but which address other problems does not imply otherwise.

CONTENTS

TABLES

INTRODUCTION

In our previous book, *Dual Diagnosis: Counseling the Mentally Ill Substance Abuser,* we provided the counselor with a comprehensive discussion of issues pertaining to the assessment and treatment of the dually diagnosed client. Now, with this workbook, we provide a therapeutic tool to assist the counselor doing Twelve Step work with the dually diagnosed client.

This workbook discusses individuals with coexisting psychiatric and substance abuse problems. We believe that the dually diagnosed client has simultaneous or *coexisting* disorders. Which disorder is *primary* can lead to lively but unproductive debate about the treatment priorities and serves little more purpose than discussion of which came first, the chicken or the egg? We believe that simultaneous treatment is necessary for the client to recover from *both* disorders. The Twelve Steps of Alcoholics Anonymous (AA) are fundamental to our treatment model.

It is not our intention to *alter* the Twelve Steps. We believe the Twelve Steps of Alcoholics Anonymous are an inspired work collectively developed by Dr. Bob, Bill W., and other early members of Alcoholics Anonymous.

We believe participation in Twelve Step recovery is the only consistently proven method to obtain and maintain quality sobriety. We also believe Twelve Step recovery tools can be used effectively with the dually diagnosed client. However, grave emotional and mental disorders can interfere with a person's ability to understand and effectively use the Twelve Steps unless the Steps are specially tailored to clients with specific disorders and the counselor uses special counseling approaches. This workbook provides a description of various serious mental and emotional disorders as well as treatment tips and modified Twelve Step work to assist the counselor in doing more effective work with dually diagnosed clients.

How to Use This Workbook

We have designed this workbook to aid counselors in doing Twelve Step work with dually diagnosed clients. Each chapter describes one of eight different psychiatric disorders. In each chapter, we offer a brief review of the psychopathology and worldview of the client with that particular diagnosis. We also provide a table (as necessary) that breaks down various elements, such as feelings, thinking, behavior, interpersonal relations and role functioning, and chemical use typical of clients with the disorder being discussed.

In some chapters, each table is followed by specialized Step-work handouts that take into account assets and limitations of the different psychiatric disorders. Traditional Twelve Step work booklets* can be used with clients diagnosed with a major depression, an anxiety disorder, or a passive-aggressive personality disorder; therefore, no specialized handouts follow these chapters.

We have developed our Step-work handouts as a suggested way that you can gather information; you are welcome to photocopy and use them with your clients. If clients need more room to write, the reverse side of a photocopied page can be used, or additional paper can be provided.

On the bottom left-hand corner of each handout there is a code. Each code is meant to help you easily identify which handouts belong to which disorder once the handouts are photocopied and thus separated from the chapter to which they belong. Excluding those chapters without handouts, the key is as follows:

SZ — Schizophrenia
BP — Bipolar Disorder
OM — Organic Mental Disorder
AS — Anti-Social Personality Disorder
BL — Borderline Personality Disorder

Before we give out the Step-work handouts to our dually diagnosed clients, we make sure they have a basic conceptual understanding of the first three Steps, or in the case of some of the personality disorders, the first four Steps.

Toward the end of this workbook, you'll find a Comments for Facilitators section (page 105) where we have provided some key concepts and things to watch out for when working with dually diagnosed clients in specific Step-work handouts. The Twelve Steps of Alcoholics Anonymous in their entirety are also at the back of this workbook (page 113).

---

*Hazelden Educational Materials offers a number of pamphlets and workbooks dealing with the Twelve Steps.

CHAPTER ONE

SCHIZOPHRENIA

A great challenge to the treatment professional is the chemically dependent client suffering from schizophrenia. The cardinal features of schizophrenia are substantial impairment of the client's thought processes and the bizarre content of his or her thoughts. People with schizophrenia have a difficult time paying attention and understanding and applying a general principle to a particular situation. Persons with this disorder are, in a sense, learning disabled. The condition also tends to be chronic, with flare-ups in response to stress, failure to take neuroleptic medications, or chemical use. Individuals suffering from chronic schizophrenia often lead an isolated, impoverished lifestyle, making it difficult to motivate them for treatment. Table One on page 5 lists significant features of the schizophrenic disorder.

> There are three key issues in counseling schizophrenic clients: medication, activities of daily living, and socialization.

First, clients must take medication regularly to control their psychotic symptoms. Trade names of some commonly used anti-psychotic medications include Haldol, Navane, Prolixin, Stelazine, Thorazine, and Trilafon. People with schizophrenia often stop taking their medications. Sometimes it's because the side effects of the medication are uncomfortable. Sometimes they are suspicious of the medication or remain unconvinced that they are ill. Or sometimes they become so disorganized that nothing gets done in a routine fashion.

Second, people with schizophrenia often must have assistance performing activities of daily living, including eating, grooming, and attending scheduled events such as clinic appointments.

Finally, they need to engage in activities that increase social contact with others.

Think structure, structure, structure. Written prompts such as checklists of daily living activities and hour-by-hour time schedules are useful. Even with these aids, the person with schizophrenia will benefit from supervision by a case manager who can remind, prompt, assist, and praise the client. Many of these clients will require on-the-spot supervision in a residential home placement or day treatment program. Keep this in mind when helping them do Step work or urging AA or Narcotics Anonymous (NA) attendance and aftercare activities.

When stable, people with schizophrenia benefit from socialization activities. This keeps them oriented and involved with others; hence they receive support for coping with their illness. Attendance at AA or NA can help meet this need.

People with schizophrenia have trouble hearing new information and translating it into new behavior. Use lots of visual aids and attention-getting devices such as exaggerated emphasis with the voice, shifts of position, and numerous hand movements during classes. Keep material simple and concrete and repeat it several times. Help the client apply new materials to each specific situation. It is helpful to demonstrate the behavior; then ask the client to role-play the behavior.

> **S**tudies suggest that clients with schizophrenia use more stimulants, cannabis, hallucinogens, inhalants, caffeine, and tobacco — and use less alcohol, opiates, and sedative-hypnotics — than other clients.[1]

In our experience, rates of alcohol and marijuana use are high because these drugs are easily accessible. If there is *any* report of chemical use, even "just" alcohol or marijuana, the client needs dual diagnosis treatment. *Any* use of alcohol and drugs is *contra-indicated* for the person with schizophrenia because chemicals intensify symptoms and decrease compliance with treatment.

Marijuana is a real problem. Our own clinical experience is that people with schizophrenia who smoke marijuana, even when taking proper doses of medication, often experience a psychotic episode. When abusing alcohol, they tend to discontinue taking medication since the alcohol further disorganizes them and exacerbates side effects of the medication. They sometimes abuse their side effect medication because of the "buzz" that anti-cholinergic agents like Artane and Cogentin can deliver. Watch out for schizophrenic clients who run out of their side effect medication before their anti-psychotic medication. They could be using (or selling) the anti-cholinergic medication. Constantly distinguish a medication from a drug and support compliance with properly taking prescribed medication and staying abstinent from alcohol and other drugs.

2

Just like other alcohol and other drug abusers, people with schizophrenia often deny the effects of alcohol and other drugs on their lives. However, pounding on their denial through heavy confrontation is not appropriate. Strong confrontation will lead to further exacerbation of psychotic symptoms. Instead, the task of the recovery counselor is to slowly and painfully build into the client's worldview that he or she is chemically dependent and can't use alcohol or other drugs, ever, under any circumstances. Explaining that chemical dependency is a disease gives people with schizophrenia a concrete rationale for abstinence. If we can convince them that they are chemically dependent and need to be abstinent, we're satisfied with our work. We do not expect them to complete the first five Steps in the first thirty days of sobriety.

About the Step-Work Handouts in This Chapter . . .

The schizophrenic client will set the pace. You need to follow. Concrete, reality-based responses to Step work will indicate that he or she has integrated the concept of abstinence. We have modified our Step work for the person with schizophrenia. Our Step One focuses on unmanageability. We are clear and concrete. We stay away from too much emphasis on powerlessness because this can lead to further disorganization in the thinking of this population.

We ask schizophrenic clients to develop two sets of index cards as part of their Step One work. We first educate them on the differences between medications (good) and drugs (bad). We then assist them in writing out three reasons why they should be clean and sober on one card, and three reasons why they should take their medication on a second card. Often these reasons are very basic, such as "I'll end up in a hospital" or "I'll lose my housing." We suggest that they carry these index cards with them at all times and review them with their counselors and on their own.

In working Step Two with schizophrenic clients, it is important to maintain the here-and-now attitude developed in Step One. Abstract concepts like Higher Power tend to distract them from the goal of Step Two. Our goal in this Step is to assist them in developing the *faith* and *hope* that they need to build productive lives.

In Step Three work, as in Step Two, we minimize the discussion of Higher Power. Our goal with Step Three is to help clients identify other people, places, or things that can be helpful to them in their recovery process. Schizophrenic clients need to learn to reach out for help from appropriate people who can assist them in remaining sober and stable. While we would love to assist clients with developing a stronger spiritual program and a clear sense of who their Higher Power is, we have found that their psychotic symptoms prevent this from occurring.

Schizophrenic clients benefit from a sympathetic AA group. The counselor should be familiar with AA groups that are more tolerant of medication use and potentially disruptive behavior. AA groups frequented by chronic alcoholics can be a great support for people with schizophrenia, who often fit in quite well with people who are impaired from years of alcohol abuse and may find satisfying roles emptying ashtrays, setting up chairs, and making coffee. The counselor should warn the person with schizophrenia that some individuals might question his or her use of medication. Help the client develop responses for people who do so. We suggest helping the client get a supportive AA sponsor who can meet with both the counselor and the client to discuss the medication issue.

Comments for facilitators regarding Step work for the client with schizophrenia appear on pages 105-106.

TABLE ONE
SCHIZOPHRENIA

Feelings	Thinking	Behavior	Interpersonal Relations And Role Functioning	Chemical Use
• generally inappropriate or muted • sometimes depressed, angry, or anxious	• confusion • difficulty concentrating • concrete and unable to generalize information • bizarre content, delusions • hallucinations • greater impairment in auditory modalities	• disorganized • decreased responsiveness to others • eccentric • poor self-care	• withdrawn and isolated • poor role functioning • may be able to do low-pressure jobs not requiring public contact	• polysubstance abuse, but will abuse chemicals, such as ETOH or pot, that are easy to get • less use of opiates, sedative-hypnotics

STEP ONE

"We admitted we were powerless over alcohol — that our lives had become unmanageable."

PART 1

Give two examples of problems you *now* have that are related to your drinking and use of other drugs.

PART 2

Give two examples of trouble you have gotten into because of your drinking and use of other drugs.

PART 3

Please check the following that you feel apply to you.

_____ People tell me I drink or use other drugs too much.

_____ Others get mad at me when I drink or use other drugs.

_____ I've tried to stop drinking or using other drugs before but started up again.

_____ Sometimes I drink or use other drugs more than I planned.

SZ

STEP TWO

"Came to believe that a Power greater than ourselves could restore us to sanity."

PART 1

Give one example of how things are getting better since you stopped drinking or using other drugs.

PART 2

Give one example of someone who has been of help to you and explain why.

PART 3

Please check which of the following applied to you when you were drinking or using other drugs.

_____ I lied to my friends or family.
_____ I stole or took things that didn't belong to me.
_____ I had fights or arguments with people.
_____ Friends or family didn't want me around them when I was drinking or using other drugs.

SZ

STEP THREE

"Made a decision to turn our will and our lives over to the care of God as we understood Him."

PART 1

Give one example of something you now worry about.

PART 2

Give one example of a person you think is helpful to you or you could trust at least a little.

PART 3

How can it help you to "turn it over" or discuss this worry or problem with the person you trust?

SZ

CHAPTER TWO

BIPOLAR DISORDER (MANIC-DEPRESSION)

Bipolar disorder is a more recent term for manic-depressive illness. The primary features of a bipolar disorder are extreme swings of mood and behavior ranging from manic-euphoria and hyperactivity to depressed sadness and immobility. Some clients have only manic episodes, but most will have a history of both kinds of swings or will go on to have both. In addition, some clients will appear for treatment only during depressed episodes because they enjoy the highs too much or because the highs are only mild (hypomania) and do not lead to major difficulties. Table Two on page 12 lists key symptoms and problems for the manic phase; Table Three, which we place on page 26 at the end of Chapter Three on Major Depression, describes the depressed phase.

A key issue for the bipolar client is medication compliance. Bipolar disorder is a disorder of brain chemistry. Lithium (sometimes supplemented by an anti-psychotic during the acute phase) generally controls the symptoms very well. However, many bipolar clients like the highs (while dreading the lows) and often stop taking their medications. Other bipolar clients tell us they stopped taking their medications because they felt they were doing just fine and decided they didn't need their medications. Also, clients on lithium require routine blood draws to determine blood levels. These can be annoying for people with bipolar disorder and can be a constant reminder of their "abnormality." Educating them about their illness and the need for medications is often effective in maintaining compliance, but some clients require case management-type monitoring to help them stay on medications. As with people with schizophrenia, discussion of "good" drugs (medication) and "bad" drugs is important.

Another important issue for people with bipolar disorder is their need for grief work. Many stabilize only to find they have had multiple sexual encounters, spent all the family's money, and alienated everyone with, for example, their talk of calling the President and sharing a new idea they have for saving the United States. They need to accept their losses, repair and make amends where they can, and let go of the rest.

If not angry and threatening, manic clients can be fun to work with, but only for short periods. Their enthusiasm, energy, and giddy mood is infectious but ultimately tiring. As a rule, we avoid any attempt to stop the manic behavior. Instead we try to redirect their energy into such things as taking notes (often copious) during meetings or encouraging fast pacing up and down a hallway. Sometimes lowering stimulation levels with brief time-outs, or making sure there is no loud music, is useful. We limit the client to five minutes air-time in group per comment, permit no more than three air-times a group, and require him or her to be seated. We establish hand signals or cue words with the client to get him or her to slow down or terminate lengthy or rambling monologues.

People with bipolar disorder have a strong tendency to abuse chemicals. Mania, like chemical dependency, is a good example of out-of-control behavior. Together, mania and chemical dependency are a dangerous combination. These clients abuse all kinds of chemicals but seem to show a special fondness for stimulants to keep the manic high going, and alcohol to help them sleep.[1] The fact that they accelerate their chemical use during the manic phase has led to the mistaken belief that they are only self-medicating and that just controlling the mania will eliminate the chemical abuse problem. We have seen numbers of bipolar clients who can't stop abusing alcohol or other drugs between episodes and whose failure to abstain contributes to another acute episode of their bipolar illness. We are not aware of any immunity of this population to chemical dependency.

We ask that the manic client's responses to chemical dependency lectures and Step work be clear, concise, and as reality-based as possible. We respond with gentle but firm limit-setting to such things as fifty written pages of run-on sentences, designation of themselves as the Higher Power, and attempts to rewrite the Twelve Steps. As their lithium levels approach the therapeutic range, the clients will become better to work with. The recovery approach can help them deal not only with their chemical dependency, but also their bipolar illness. Both are diseases; both involve issues of out-of-control behavior; both provide a way of doing grief work and repairing the personal and interpersonal damage associated with these diseases. Examples of Step work specialized for the manic client can be found at the end of this chapter.

About the Step-Work Handouts in This Chapter . . .

In working Step One with manic clients, it is important to try to get them to be concrete and succinct in their responses. Keep them oriented toward ways their drinking or using made their lives unmanageable. Specific examples with limited explanations are the most helpful. Discussions of power and control need to be kept to a minimum, as clients tend to become quite grandiose and expansive on philosophical issues.

Step Two for these manic clients also needs to be clear and concise. Keep long explanations to a minimum and discussions of Higher Power on hold. Extended dialogues will only lead them further away from a grounded recovery.

We do not ask manic clients to give explanations for each "mistake in thinking" on Part One of Step Two in the same way we do the anti-social client (as explained in Chapter Seven). Our goal is to get them to see their own denial. Lengthy explanations tend to lead them into intellectual rambling. Readers may want to review the thinking errors material in Chapter Seven (Table Seven, pages 53-56) to further understand the notion of denial as "mistakes in thinking."

Step Three provides these clients with the opportunity to identify others who can be helpful to them. Learning to identify an appropriate support system and asking others to help them is essential. Manic clients who have a grandiose sense of self need to acknowledge that there are others who know more than they do and who have the expertise to help them. We keep the Higher Power concept on a concrete level so as not to lead them down a path that is not reality-based.

We encourage manic clients to get involved in AA and to get a sponsor. We help structure these interactions so that they learn boundaries and don't burn out a well-meaning sponsor with eight phone calls a day, or monopolize AA meetings with lengthy, rambling speeches on spirituality.

Comments for facilitators regarding Step work for the client with a bipolar disorder (manic depression) appear on pages 106-107.

TABLE TWO
MANIA

Feeling	Thinking	Behavior	Interpersonal Relations And Role Functioning	Chemical Use
• euphoric, up, high • sometimes irritable, angry, especially when blocked by others • often a history of severe depression	• grandiose, unrealistically optimistic • racing thoughts • distractible	• hyperactive • decreased sleep • flamboyant, loud, outrageous manner • many projects, reckless activity	• conflict with family, authority, anyone saying no • decreased functioning during acute episodes • very often good functioning between episodes	• polysubstance abuse and dependency, use of alcohol during highs • use of stimulants during highs and lows

STEP ONE

"We admitted we were powerless over alcohol — that our lives had become unmanageable."

PART 1

List three examples of how you have gotten into trouble because of drinking and using other drugs (no more than 100 words each).

PART 2

Give two examples of "rules" you have about drinking or using other drugs that you developed in order to try to control your drinking or your use of other drugs (no more than 25 words each).

PART 3

Give one example of how you have had to modify, change, or break each of the rules in Part 2 in order to continue to drink or use other drugs (no more than 25 words each).

BP

STEP TWO

"Came to believe that a Power greater than ourselves could restore us to sanity."

PART 1

Check which of the following mistakes in thinking you used to justify your continued use of alcohol and other drugs despite problems you were having.

———— Excuse making
———— Blaming
———— Justifying
———— Super-optimism
———— Lying
———— Threatening others
———— Presenting false image
———— Building up self
———— Assuming
———— "I'm unique"
———— Grandiose thinking
———— Intellectualizing
———— Playing victim
———— Exaggerating
———— Redefining
———— Minimizing
———— Ingratiating
———— Hostile and angry outbursts
———— Making fools of others

PART 2

Give two examples of how your drinking or other drug use was "insane" (no more than 50 words each).

PART 3

Give two examples of how your life has improved since you stopped drinking or using other drugs (no more than 50 words each).

STEP THREE

"Made a decision to turn our will and our lives over to the care of God as we understood Him."

PART 1

Give two brief examples of how you tried to control your behavior and failed (no more than 50 words each).

(Step Three, continued)

PART 2

Give two brief examples of situations in which you tried to control someone else's behavior and failed (no more than 50 words each).

PART 3

Give two examples of people who have been or could be helpful to you (no more than 25 words each).

BP

(Step Three, continued)

PART 4

Give two examples of current problems you are having and describe how "turning it over" or talking with a helpful or trusted person would strengthen your recovery and reduce your anxiety (no more than 100 words each).

CHAPTER THREE

MAJOR DEPRESSION

AUTHORS' NOTE: We have not included specialized Step-work handouts in this chapter because we have found traditional Twelve Step work booklets are quite effective to use with a client who has a major depression, when incorporating the special focus we will discuss in this chapter.

The client with a major depression can be a source of conflict between mental health and chemical dependency professionals. Most newly recovering addicts and alcoholics meet the diagnostic criteria for major depression. Physiological depletion and a life increasingly out of control and littered with losses would make most people depressed. Abstinence and beginning a Twelve Step recovery program will usually clear most of these depressions in a matter of a few weeks.[1] However, there are some individuals who suffer from coexisting major depression and substance abuse.[2] These individuals do not find emotional and psychological relief from their depression through Twelve Step recovery programs alone. They require additional treatment for their coexisting disorder.

The primary feature of major depression is an intense, lasting mood characterized by blue, sad, and down feelings and accompanied by a severe lack of enjoyment of pleasurable activities. Major depression does not involve sadness due to the death of a loved one, or a discrete, one-time response to a stressor such as losing a job. Table Three at the end of this chapter (page 26) outlines typical symptoms and problems associated with major depression.

One important subtype of major depression is the melancholic (endogenous) subtype. The *DSM-III-R* diagnostic criteria[3] for the melancholic subtype includes:

1. Loss of interest or pleasure in all or most activities.
2. Lack of reactivity to usually pleasurable stimuli.
3. Depression regularly worse in the morning.
4. Early morning awakening.
5. Observable psychomotor retardation (slowing) or agitation.
6. Anorexia or weight loss.

7. No significant personality disturbance before the first episode.
8. One or more previous episodes with total or almost total recovery.
9. Previously positive responses to specific and adequate somatic anti-depressant therapy.

Five or more of the above indicators suggest a melancholic depression with substantial physiological components that respond to, and benefit from, medication or other medical intervention. One useful way of thinking about an endogenous depression is to make a distinction between the social reinforcers (fun activities, socializing, job or school performance) and biological reinforcers (food, sleep, movement, or sex). Melancholic depression involves the loss of positive, reinforcing properties of both social *and* biological reinforcers, and somatic therapies such as medication are very often necessary for treatment to be effective.

Another significant subtype is a major depression experienced by someone with a personality disorder.

Our phrase to describe this is a "personality disorder in crisis." These depressions typically involve a strong cognitive component of hopelessness, poor morale, and suicidal ideation, and they represent the failure of long-standing ways of dealing with the world. The anti-social personality, for example, will sometimes experience brief but profound depression when put in jail, an "I got caught" depression. While these depressions are legitimate and require management, the long-term focus needs to be the personality disorder, and the treatment of choice is psychotherapy. Medication is generally not indicated.

Some depressions can assume psychotic proportions, and the various subtypes are not mutually exclusive. Careful observation and a thorough history are essential to establish the diagnosis of depression and the subtype, especially when dealing with the depressed, dually diagnosed person. A conservative (wait-and-see) approach is warranted with most dually diagnosed clients. Some individuals will require active treatment for a coexisting major depression. All depressed people need assessment for suicide potential and intervention if necessary.

Increasing the activity rate and decreasing negative thoughts of depressed people are important treatment objectives. We like to pinpoint potentially pleasant activities with clients and help them engage in these activities. A discussion about the fact that a positive mood comes from doing pleasant or constructive activities can help challenge the faulty thinking of many depressed persons, which is *I need to* feel *good before I can* do *good*. Making lists of positive attributes and accomplishments and encouraging clients to engage in scheduled positive self-talk sessions are other ways to combat the negative thinking prevalent in major depression.

The service provider can also gently challenge the reality basis of clients' cognitive distortions such as *It's all my fault. . . . Nothing will ever be better. . . . Things are grim and will get worse.* Global negative thinking is not helpful to the depressed person.

Building or rebuilding social support systems is a crucial component of treatment for people with a major depression.

Whether cause or effect or both, an important target for treatment must often be the depressed person's impoverished or conflicted social support system. Many of these people also lack development in social skills and benefit from such interventions as assertion training. Stressful events often trigger depression, and stress management skills are often helpful in coping with current and future stressors.

We use a kind but firm approach with seriously depressed individuals and push for more healthy behavior. Gentle insistence is often effective with this population, as is setting time limits for complaint sessions, "poor me's," and other unhelpful behavior. Keep in mind that many seriously depressed people have trouble concentrating and are more impaired in the visual-motor channels. Use auditory input; ask them to give you summaries back; and be prepared to repeat information.

Dually diagnosed people with a major depression present a variety of patterns of chemical use in our experience. They tend to abuse sedatives, tranquilizers, and alcohol. Older individuals tend to abuse alcohol or anti-anxiety agents, while young clients evidence more polysubstance use. This reflects the trends in the general population. Given the mixture of depression subtypes, the lack of distinct trends should not be surprising.

> **D**o not be too quick to relieve the chemically dependent person's depression that stems from grief over losses due to his or her use.

"Grief" depression allows a window through denial; thus, the chemically dependent client can see him- or herself realistically. Step work and other components of a good recovery program will help resolve this grief. Needless to say, abstinence is necessary for recovery to occur.

A moderately depressed person without melancholic symptoms who is abusing chemicals may require just a good program for recovery from chemical dependency to help their depression. The support network provided by AA, the reframing of thoughts provided by the disease concept (*sick getting well*, not *bad getting good*), the structured activities of

Twelve Step work, and the practice of expressing feelings in a direct, honest manner can all be effective antidotes for depression.

Severe depression with either a high risk of suicide or melancholic symptoms requires a dual diagnosis approach. Management of the potential for suicide by setting up safety watches with family members or hospitalizing the client is required. Medication for melancholic symptoms is necessary. Educating the person about the need for medication and finding sympathetic AA groups is helpful.

We have not found it necessary to modify our Twelve Step work with the depressed client; therefore, no Step-work handouts are included at the end of this chapter. We do, however, put a strong emphasis on the strengths and assets of depressed persons, and don't allow them to beat themselves up over past behaviors. We may also augment their recovery work with referral to a psychiatrist with dual diagnosis expertise. This professional contact can evaluate the need for antidepressant medication and whether a similarly experienced mental health professional for psychotherapy should be involved.

> **W**hile we have not found it necessary to develop specialized Step work for the depressed client, we do have some suggestions that may prove helpful.

A solid Step One is crucial for depressed clients. They must learn to let go of control. They are consumed by sadness and grief and have become self-absorbed in their melancholic worldview. They feel responsible for all the world's problems. Step One offers clients the opportunity to learn to let go of trying to control the uncontrollable. By admitting *powerlessness*, they can become free to begin emptying the heavy load they have carried with them for so long. We try to focus on *powerlessness* and *surrender* rather than on *unmanageability* with these clients. Depressed people are experts in beating themselves up for the "mistakes" they've made and the "bad" things they have done. We want to help them see the paradox of Step One: by admitting powerlessness, they are improved and set free to go about the job of living life one day at a time.

Step Two is a step of faith. Depressed people have to some degree lost hope that anyone or anything can be helpful to them. By *coming to believe*, they step out of the problem and into the solution.

Step Three offers depressed individuals a way to let go of their defeating and negative self-talk. By assisting them in discovering a reasonable and helpful Higher Power they understand, Step Three allows them to see that there is help for them. This is the lesson of Step Two and Three. Step

Three is an opportunity for action. By learning to "turn it over" and "let go and let God" depressed clients learn that there is clear action available. They begin to experience glimpses of serenity; they begin to know peace.

With appropriate treatment, the chances of recovery for the depressed, dually diagnosed person are excellent. The challenge for the treatment provider is determining the appropriate treatment and making sure these clients understand they have two diseases — chemical dependency *and* depression. Abstinence alone will not remove the major depression, and psychotherapy and antidepressants alone won't eliminate substance abuse.

TABLE THREE
MAJOR DEPRESSION

Feeling	Thinking	Behavior	Interpersonal Relations And Role Functioning	Chemical Use
• down, blue, sad • sometimes irritable	• diminished ability to concentrate, make decisions • helpless or hopeless mind-set • guilty feelings • thoughts of death and dying, self-harm • may have delusions in severe cases • serious confusion in some older clients	• apathetic and slowed down, decreased activity • may have decreased eating and sleeping, occasionally increased eating and sleeping • may be agitated • acting out in some adolescents	• withdrawn, isolated • decreased functioning during episodes	• polysubstance abuse and dependency • heavy use of alcohol and other depressant drugs

CHAPTER FOUR

ANXIETY DISORDERS

AUTHORS' NOTE: We have not included specialized Step work in this chapter because we have found traditional Twelve Step work booklets are quite effective to use with a client who has an anxiety disorder, when incorporating the special focus we will discuss in this chapter.

The cardinal features of anxiety disorders are bodily stress and avoidance of the anxiety-provoking situation. Table Four at the end of this chapter (page 31) outlines additional features of this set of disorders. Under the general category of anxiety disorders falls a number of specific conditions:

- Panic disorder with or without agoraphobia
- Agoraphobia
- Social phobia
- Simple phobia
- Obsessive-compulsive disorder
- Post-traumatic stress disorder
- Generalized anxiety disorder

Counselors interested in the exact diagnostic criteria for each should refer to the *DSM-III-R*.[1] Generally, a useful distinction for thinking about these disorders is the degree to which there is a specific focus on the trigger for the anxiety. These triggers range from specific phobias through agoraphobia (fear of being in places where escape is difficult or help is not available) up to the anxious-all-the-time feeling of generalized anxiety disorder. The more focused the trigger, the less incapacitating the disorder is for the client and the more relevant are specific behavioral interventions.

Another useful distinction is between the phobias and other anxiety disorders. There is some evidence suggesting that more general anxiety disorders may be related to major affective illness, and anti-depressant medication seems to be helpful.[2,3] We believe in a careful assessment, including objective psychological testing, to support our clinical opinion prior to referring a dually diagnosed person for any medication.

Not surprisingly, alcohol and other sedative-hypnotics are commonly abused in this population. Medical professionals unfamiliar with dual diagnosis issues often prescribe anti-anxiety agents for individuals presenting these disorders. This runs the risk of establishing an addiction, provoking relapse, or creating an additional addiction because of the cross-addictive qualities of these kinds of medications. In addition, it promotes the false assumption in clients that the cure to their distress lies outside of themselves. Taking a pill to fix things is an easy way to avoid the self-exploration and active coping necessary for long-term recovery from an anxiety disorder. The focus needs to be on psychotherapeutic strategies and perhaps the use of non-addictive medication.

> **G**enerally, we like to teach the patient anxiety management skills such as relaxation techniques, positive self-talk, and imagery.

We combine anxiety management skills with gradual exposure to the feared situation and prevention of the avoidance response. For a client with post-traumatic stress disorder, working through the traumatic memories in a safe, supportive setting is often helpful. These settings can include support groups, outpatient therapy groups or, in extreme situations, inpatient settings. Aerobic exercise often is beneficial, as is appropriate nutrition. The provider will need to assess the family and intervene where needed. We also see high rates of codependency and other marital difficulties in this population, and feel strongly that these issues need to be assessed and treated as necessary. Codependents trying to "manage the unmanageable," including an addicted family member, will be anxious. In fact, our experience indicates that whether cause or effect, many persons with anxiety disorders are in relationships that have codependent features.

We use a gentle but firm approach to encourage clients with anxiety disorders to cope one step at a time, one day at a time. Directing these clients to focus, repeating material, and frequently checking for comprehension helps deal with concentration difficulties. Except with severe cases, most of these clients can be managed on an outpatient basis.

Chemical dependency counselors need to recognize the special issues associated with panic disorders. When suggesting attendance at AA meetings, the counselor should understand the acute fear of large groups that these clients experience and make provisions for this. Small, intimate AA meetings are helpful. A counselor, sponsor, or supportive family member may want to accompany a client to his or her first few meetings.

Step work needs to emphasize the synergistic quality of substance abuse with anxiety disorders. The use of minor tranquilizers such as Valium or Xanax can, with prolonged use, actually *increase* agitation and paranoia and can interfere with psychotherapy.[4,5] The concept of powerlessness in Step One needs to emphasize the paradox of this Step. By accepting that they are not in control of their alcohol or other drug use, and by accepting that their attempts to control the uncontrollable has only led to loss of control, anxious people can begin to achieve serenity.

The first three Steps of AA assist the client in letting go of strong control issues and developing a calmer "what will be, will be" attitude. The growth of a sense of faith occurring in Step Two can help the anxiety disordered individual begin to believe that "things eventually go the way they are supposed to" and that "all my worrying does is upset me: it doesn't change people, places, or things."

The Twelve Steps of AA were designed for anxious, guilty, and depressed people. For this reason, we have not found it necessary to develop special Step-work handouts for anxiety disorders. For the more extreme anxiety disorders — panic disorder, post-traumatic stress disorder, and agoraphobia — we do have pointers that may prove helpful.

Step One offers the anxiety disordered client an opportunity to let go and surrender attempts to stay in control. Like the depressed person, the anxiety disordered person needs to learn how much freedom there is by admitting "I'm not in control" or "I've made a mistake." Many anxious clients become consumed with the need for perfection and trying not to make any mistakes. Making mistakes is seen as failure and proves they are bad people.

> **B**y understanding they are *sick getting well*, not *bad getting good*, anxiety disordered clients can begin to acknowledge their *two* diseases: the addiction *and* the anxiety disorder. The chemically dependent, anxious person should focus on the unmanageability of his or her disease, but not be allowed to obsess or focus too much on "how bad I've been."

Step Two offers anxious clients the chance to discover someone or something that can be helpful to them. When discussing issues around the "insanity" of their diseases, we use the definition of *insanity* as repeating the same mistakes and expecting different results.

Step Three is an opportunity to learn to let go of control and let things work out the way they are supposed to.

We work these Steps concurrently on both the substance abuse and the anxiety disorder. Our clients may identify themselves as "I'm Connie and I'm a recovering addict and an agoraphobic." Knowing *what* diseases they have allows clients to move on to *who* they are.

Working the Twelve Steps assists these persons in developing personal responsibility for recovery. One way of demonstrating personal responsibility is for clients to inform their physicians (in writing) of their addiction and their need for abstinence. This strategy is useful for dealing with the widespread prescription drug dependence found among these clients.

In our experience, persons with anxiety disorders are at significant risk for relapse. Many of these individuals experience residual symptoms of anxiety, and this tempts them to seek relief by renewed use of chemicals or by the use of compulsive behaviors such as overeating, gambling, and so on. Counselors need to monitor their anxious clients for relapse or new problem behaviors, and insist that their clients develop an ongoing, long-term recovery program to ensure success.

TABLE FOUR
ANXIETY DISORDERS

Feeling	Thinking	Behavior	Interpersonal Relations And Role Functioning	Chemical Use
• tension, fearfulness, discomfort, panic	• worry • difficulty concentrating • flashbacks, intrusive thoughts of tension • blocking of thoughts	• avoidance of feared situations • hypervigilance • bodily symptoms	• withdrawal, isolation • detachment from others • decreased role functioning	• polysubstance abuse and dependency • some preference for alcohol and other sedative-hypnotics, may use cocaine in an attempt to achieve euphoria

CHAPTER FIVE

ORGANIC MENTAL DISORDERS

The essential feature of an organic mental disorder is a psychological or behavioral abnormality associated with transient or permanent dysfunction of the brain and judged to be caused by a specific organic factor.

The term *organic mental disorder* encompasses an enormous variety of symptoms and causes. Symptoms can be relatively global as in a dementia, where many different cognitive and behavioral difficulties exist. Other disorders entail more specific symptoms, such as organic hallucinosis with its vivid and persistent hallucinations. The disorder can be acute as with a delirium due to an active infection, or with toxification (a kind of delirium) due to recent use of psychoactive or other chemicals. The course can also be chronic as with a dementia due to head injury or with such diseases as Alzheimer's. Finally, the presenting symptoms can include obvious cognitive problems, such as difficulty remembering recent events and the inability to care for oneself, to more subtle disturbances of mood and behavior. An example of a more subtle organic mental disorder is organic personality disorder, with its outbursts and inappropriate behavior, or marked indifference and apathy.

We will limit our discussion in this chapter to more chronic organic mental disorders due to chemical use, and to the mild to moderate dementias, whatever the cause. Delirium, acute withdrawal, severe toxification, as well as severe dementia require medical and nursing management to ensure safety and health.

Some chemically abusing or dependent individuals can evidence a prolonged withdrawal syndrome.[1] Anxiety, depression, cognitive difficulties, physical symptoms, irritability and emotional lability, and transient psychotic symptoms (frequently associated with amphetamine or cocaine abuse) can characterize this syndrome. Withdrawal from alcohol and, most especially, sedatives, such as the benzodiazepines, can also produce such states. Counselors have reported benzodiazepine withdrawal psychosis in clients as late as fourteen days after the beginning of abstinence. Cessation of stimulant or hallucinogenic drugs often causes a prolonged withdrawal syndrome characterized by serious depression, as well as irritability and anxiety. This appears to be especially true of cocaine and crack users. The existence of a prolonged withdrawal syndrome associated with marijuana is controversial, but our clinical experience has convinced us that chronic pot smokers do experience such difficulties.

Occasionally, people will show an especially severe prolonged withdrawal syndrome marked by psychosis, or assaultive or suicidal behavior, and will require higher levels of care and the diagnostic abilities a dual diagnosis program can offer.

One phenomena of interest is a long-lasting, schizophrenic-like condition that persists after prolonged and heavy stimulant or hallucinogen use. Investigators have suggested that the phenomena of "kindling" might account for this particular condition, which is characterized by psychotic symptoms, but with social approach behavior intact.[2] Stimulants and hallucinogens appear to produce their effects in the same brain tracts that are associated with schizophrenia. According to this model, chronic stimulant or hallucinogen use appear to produce permanently damaged, easily stimulated neurons in these tracts that account for this schizophrenic-like condition. Other research suggests a genetic component for this condition.[3] This schizophrenic-like condition can last months or years and requires interventions similar to those used with schizophrenia. However, in our experience, these individuals are more amenable to treatment than many people with schizophrenia, because they bring personal strengths and skills to the treatment (including ease in relating to other people) not always found with persons suffering from a schizophrenic condition. Individuals with this schizophrenic-like disorder also tend to have a profound sense of the losses caused by their chemical use. This makes working through denial somewhat easier.

Dementia is the prototypical organic mental disorder that raises the issue of the need for dual diagnosis treatment.

The essential features of dementia are memory difficulties and other cognitive impairments, as well as profound personality deterioration. Table Five (page 37) presents the signs and symptoms of dementia in more detail.

Chronic alcoholism leads to a progressive deterioration of cognitive abilities. This deterioration occurs surprisingly early (as soon as thirty years of age) and seems related more to amounts consumed in one sitting than to frequency and duration of alcohol use. Alcoholism causes impaired non-verbal abstract thinking and visual-motor slowing, as well as short- and long-term memory problems. Auditory-verbal abilities are relatively intact, but where these tasks require new learning, chronic alcoholics show difficulties in these areas as well. Some evidence exists for similar impairments among chronic users of other sedative-hypnotics. Surprisingly, the research evidence shows mixed results about whether there are significant, lasting cognitive impairments for chronic use of marijuana, opiates, amphetamines, barbiturates, and hallucinogens. The limited research on inhalant users, however, has found evidence for cognitive damage.[4]

Dementia caused by head trauma is also a common organic mental disorder among dually diagnosed clients. Some chemically dependent individuals either grew up in or are currently in family situations where physical abuse has been so severe that brain damage resulted. Other chemically dependent individuals have suffered motor vehicle accidents or falls.

Mild impairment (where judgment remains relatively intact, where the capacity for independent living remains and the performance of self-care activities is adequate, but where there are work and social difficulties) requires evaluation regarding impulse control and ability to learn at reasonable rates with standard procedures, in order to determine the need for dual diagnosis treatment. Serious learning difficulties or poor impulse control show the need for specialized dual diagnosis treatment.

Another consideration for treatment planning is the history and course of the disorder. Especially for younger persons, some recovery from traumatic head injuries is possible. Abstinence from alcohol often results in at least the partial return of cognitive abilities for those with a dementia related to alcohol abuse. On the other hand, a rapidly progressive dementia, such as early onset Alzheimer's, makes investment of time, energy, and resources in chemical dependency treatment questionable. A good rule of thumb is to determine the rate of improvement or deterioration over a six-month period and to expect little additional improvement after one year. Abstinence is essential for *any* improvement to occur.

> **W**e use many of the same general interventions for people with organic mental disorders that we use for those with schizophrenia.

The use of cueing devices such as checklists, reminder cards, and daily schedules is helpful. Keeping material simple and concrete, repeating information frequently, and applying new material and practicing new behavior on a situation-by-situation basis are also useful. Neuropsychological testing can help pinpoint strengths and weaknesses and allow counselors to fine-tune their approach. Watch out for the "talks-good-but-can't-apply-it" syndrome. Some chemically dependent clients with an organic mental disorder still have intact verbal skills, but cannot generalize concepts, deal with complexity, or tolerate frustration. When in doubt, the counselor should keep it simple and stick to one point at a time.

Abstinence is the only goal for the person with an organic mental disorder. A brain especially vulnerable to the toxic effects of chemicals and compromised in its abilities does not need more of the same.

We have found a variety of substance abuse patterns in this population. Alcohol is often the drug of choice with demented people because of ease of access. We have seen a few clients abuse phenobarbital (prescribed for a seizure disorder).

About the Step-Work Handouts in This Chapter . . .

Step work needs to be concrete and simple. We use flash cards and simple one line questions and answers with this group. Generally, the Step work we use with those who suffer from schizophrenia is most useful with this group; therefore, the Step-work handouts at the end of this chapter are identical to those in Chapter One. These clients can participate fully in AA meetings. They may need a support person to accompany them to meetings and to assure that they arrive at the right location. The support person can also help prevent clients' rambling and incoherent comments during the meeting. Non-verbal as well as verbal cueing on the part of the counselor can condition the client to develop acceptable group behavior. Going slowly, keeping it simple, and tailoring approaches to the particular clients will often result in success.

Comments for facilitators regarding Step work for the client with an organic mental disorder appear on pages 105-106.

TABLE FIVE
DEMENTIA

Feeling	Thinking	Behavior	Interpersonal Relations And Role Functioning	Chemical Use
• sometimes anxiety or depression • sometimes apathy or indifference • sometimes emotional lability and irritability	• short- and long-term memory impairment • impaired abstract thinking and judgment • impaired auditory-verbal or visual-motor abilities • sometimes paranoid thinking • slower information processing	• often poor impulse control with actions that are potentially harmful • often outbursts, tantrums, assaults • sometimes disorganized or repetitive behavior • change or exaggeration in personality style	• often increased conflict with significant others • impairment in work and social activities, poor coping with stressors • impaired activities of daily living in serious cases	• polysubstance abuse, but generally the more accessible chemicals such as alcohol or marijuana

STEP ONE

"We admitted we were powerless over alcohol — that our lives had become unmanageable."

PART 1

Give two examples of problems you *now* have that are related to your drinking and use of other drugs.

PART 2

Give two examples of trouble you have gotten into because of your drinking and use of other drugs.

PART 3

Please check the following which you feel apply to you.

_____ People tell me I drink or use other drugs too much.

_____ Others get mad at me when I drink or use other drugs.

_____ I've tried to stop drinking or using other drugs before but started up again.

_____ Sometimes I drink or use other drugs more than I planned.

OM

38

STEP TWO

"Came to believe that a Power greater than ourselves could restore us to sanity."

PART 1

Give one example of how things are getting better since you stopped drinking or using other drugs.

PART 2

Give one example of someone who has been of help to you and explain why.

PART 3

Please check which of the following applied to you when you were drinking or using other drugs.

_____ I lied to my friends or family.

_____ I stole or took things that didn't belong to me.

_____ I had fights or arguments with people.

_____ Friends or family didn't want me around them when I was drinking or using drugs.

OM

STEP THREE

"Made a decision to turn our will and our lives over to the care of God as we understood Him."

PART 1

Give one example of something you now worry about.

PART 2

Give one example of a person you think is helpful to you or you could trust at least a little.

PART 3

How can it help you to "turn it over" or discuss this worry or problem with the person you trust?

OM

CHAPTER SIX

PASSIVE-AGGRESSIVE PERSONALITY DISORDER

AUTHORS' NOTE: We have not included specialized Step-work handouts in this chapter as we have found traditional Twelve Step work booklets are quite effective to use with a client who has a passive-aggressive personality disorder, when incorporating the special focus we will discuss in this chapter.

This section of the workbook begins our discussion of chemically dependent individuals with certain coexisting personality disorders. We will focus on passive-aggressive, anti-social, and borderline personality disorders because they are relatively common and difficult to counsel. Because these disorders can be difficult to distinguish among clients who are "only" chemically dependent, and because these disorders are difficult to distinguish from each other, we have included Table Six on the next page for the reader's use. This table compares and contrasts key aspects of these three personality disorders. The reader may want to review Table Six before reading this and the following two chapters.

TABLE SIX

CHARACTERISTICS OF PASSIVE-AGGRESSIVE, ANTI-SOCIAL, AND BORDERLINE PERSONALITY DISORDERS

Area	Passive-Aggressive	Anti-Social	Borderline
Affect	overcontrolled hostility	angry intimidation	angry self-harm
Worldview	I do everything right and they still act this way	If you don't do what I want, you'll be sorry	I've got to get you before you get me
	I don't deserve this	I deserve it all	I don't deserve to exist
	I'm fine; ignore the tears	They're the ones with the problem	Help me, help me, but you can't
Presenting Problem	depression, somatizing their problems, sedative dependence, codependency	legal difficulties, poly-substance abuse and dependence, parasitic relationships	self-harm, weird thinking and behavior, episodic poly-substance abuse, hot-cold relationships
Social Functioning	consistent underachievement	episodic achievement	gross dysfunctioning
Motivation	belonging	self-esteem	safety
Defenses	repression	rationalization, projection	autistic fantasy

A main feature of the passive-aggressive personality disorder is passive resistance to required social and occupational performance.[1] Passive-aggressive individuals often lack confidence in their ability to meet their own needs and become dependent on others to provide psychological care and support. They feel direct requests and expression of negative feelings will lead to rejection and distancing by others. Often, people with passive-aggressive personalities will go above and beyond the call of duty and perform all kinds of caretaking-of-others activities in an indirect attempt to coerce love and gain acceptance. When others don't respond the "right" way (and they often don't), passive-aggressive people become chronically irritable and adopt a martyr attitude. Caught between the longing to "belong" to someone who will meet their needs, and their belief that assertive expression of feelings and needs will result in isolation, the anger of passive-aggressive people leaks out in a thousand different ways.

These are the clients who forget their counseling appointment, arrive late, or somehow just couldn't get their homework done. These are the people who control through passivity, giving little in sessions and always having an excuse.

Passive-aggressive people often present feelings of anxiety and depression as well as vague somatic complaints. The failure to obtain what they need in a consistent and direct fashion results in these negative feelings. Complaints of headaches, backaches, and other so-called functional (no medical basis) body symptoms represent an indirect way of getting attention and concern. These complaints also represent the "stuffing" of angry feelings and the resultant chronic stress.

Many passive-aggressive people will also have marital and family difficulties. Codependency is a common issue for these clients. This is not to say that all codependents are passive-aggressive. Simply, these clients often have acute codependency issues. They can be in relationships where the significant other is abusing chemicals or abusing them; yet, they will stay in the relationship, perhaps nagging the substance abuser or burning the toast, but still enabling the behavior of the significant other.

The general goal of therapy with passive-aggressive clients is to build up their sense of self and improve their sagging self-esteem. There are three ways the counselor can do this. First, bring the client together with others who will support his or her needs and who will help the client get those needs met. Therapists who suggest to certain clients the termination of an unhealthy, codependent relationship early on in therapy will trigger passive resistance. They will discover these clients will be late to appointments, or "forget" appointments altogether. These clients need the supportive alliances that stem from the therapeutic relationship, attendance at support groups, or the establishment of a friendship network.

Second, make clients aware of how their indirect ways of relating are not working. Asking open-ended questions, reviewing their relationships with others, encouraging them to read books about such topics as codependency, and gently calling them on their failure to follow through on homework assignments are useful ways of doing this.

Finally, *assertion* work can help clients understand that they have rights and can develop direct ways of relating to others.

Passive-aggressive people are at risk for developing chemical dependency, often with a preference for alcohol and sedative-hypnotics. Many come from alcoholic families, predisposing them to chemical dependency. In addition, the state induced by alcohol and sedative-hypnotics — shutting off one's feelings and the consequent lack of awareness, thereby increasing the person's repression of self — is common among people with passive-aggressive personalities. That *What bad feelings? I'll deal with it tomorrow* defense strategy is analogous to the blanking-out function served by this class of chemicals. Finally, people who are passive-aggressive are often raised to be "nice." Nice people drink at the country club or take medications their doctor prescribed; nice people don't buy heroin from a pusher.

A Twelve Step program is highly effective for these individuals. Dealing with control issues via Step work is very therapeutic. The recovery model also provides excellent social support and practice in the direct expression of feelings. When it is combined with assertion work, we have found that the package is powerful and effective. Be clear and explicit in your expectations and hold clients accountable for completing assignments. Do not accept excuses or settle for a "polite" cop-out from you or from clients. Be careful to talk about cross-addiction issues, such as between alcohol and Valium.

> **P**assive-aggressive individuals need to take responsibility for informing their physicians about their addiction to prevent further prescribing of potentially addicting substances.

We ask our clients to write letters to their doctors as part of a Step One exercise, informing their doctors of their addiction and ways they manipulated their doctors for drugs. This helps with surrender, cutting off their supply while at the same time educating their physicians. Family education and attendance at Al-Anon or Alateen also reinforce individual work with clients.

44

We have not found it necessary to develop specialized Step-work handouts for passive-aggressive clients. Traditional Twelve Step work booklets work quite nicely. Again, the key is to *hold the clients accountable.* Step work should be thorough and complete, legibly written, and handed in on time. Do not "bend the rules" for these clients, or you will find yourself (1) making promises and exceptions you don't feel good about and (2) enabling their chemical dependency and undermining their recovery.

It is critical that passive-aggressive individuals complete a thorough Step One. They need to focus on their strong need for control and how it is making their lives unmanageable. Clients are likely to gloss over negative feelings and situations when discussing unmanageability. They need a firm, supportive nudge to take a long, hard, honest look at the wreckage and unmanageability of their drug and alcohol use and their attempts to control others.

Step Two affords these people the opportunity to take a leap of faith. Clients feel that "if it weren't for me, nothing would be done correctly." Step Two is an opportunity to unburden the client from the heavy load of unnecessary responsibilities. Feeling responsible for all that goes on around you can be quite tiring. Learning to believe there is a Power greater than themselves allows passive-aggressive people to step out of the driver's seat and develop a belief in a Power who can "run" things, perhaps even better than they can. While we don't suggest any particular Higher Power, we encourage our clients to use a Higher Power that is likely to be helpful, such as God, the AA group, or the Twelve Steps.

Step Three allows these people an opportunity to release and "let go" of all obsession, worry, and fear that accompanies the passive-aggressive disorder.

> **M**aking a decision to turn one's will and life over to a Higher Power is the beginning of commitment to change. By deciding to let go of control, clients take action to develop a new program for living.

The "turning it over" aspect of Step Three allows people with passive-aggressive personalities to give their worries over to a helpful, caring Higher Power. Passive-aggressive people, with their strong dependency issues, have looked long and hard to find the "right person" who would "take care of" them. By transferring their dependency needs to the Twelve Step program and to a Higher Power, they finally have a constant source of support. Developing a belief that their Higher Power can do for them what they can't do for themselves instills a sense of hope and peace of mind seriously lacking in passive-aggressive clients' lives.

45

CHAPTER SEVEN

ANTI-SOCIAL PERSONALITY DISORDER

The key feature of the anti-social personality is a pattern of irresponsible behavior and behavior that violates the rights of others, social norms, and laws.[1] These individuals have a massively inflated sense of self, combined with total disregard for the feelings of others. The anti-social personality lacks genuine guilt or remorse over wrongful behaviors inflicted on others.

People with an anti-social personality have a distorted worldview. If you get arrested for beating up and robbing a store clerk, according to the anti-social, the problem is not *your behavior*, the problem is you got *caught!*

They believe they are never responsible; it's always someone else's fault. There is always a good reason why they did something, or at the very least, a lengthy explanation full of rationalizations. Maintenance of their inflated sense of self is a prime motivation of people with anti-social personalities, and they have an attitude of entitlement. Looking good, being cool, and being better than anyone else is their preoccupation. Their "image" is central to their psychological workings. Thrill and excitement seeking is another key motivator. Boredom is the enemy of the anti-social, and patience is not their long suit. Remember, payoffs and rewards for these clients need to be scheduled frequently — long-term goals with delayed gratification are not helpful. Finally, to people with anti-social personalities, life is a game and the object is to win, preferably in the most exciting, grandiose style possible. Even more importantly, they want others to lose and the losers to acknowledge this, even publicly.

Anti-social people sometimes get depressed, even to the point of being suicidal and making suicide attempts.[2] This depression is typically in response to getting caught by the police or otherwise suffering the negative consequences of their behavior. The depression is brief and will pass as they regroup and redefine their problems as everyone else's.

Needless to say, legal difficulties are common. Remember, it's *getting caught* that is seen as the problem by these people, *not* breaking the law or infringing on the rights of others. Marital and family difficulties are common. Generally, it's their significant other who has the complaints. People with anti-social personalities are just fine with their relationships as long as the other person meets their needs and doesn't dare presume to want anything back. Their relationships tend to be parasitic. They may use other people for status or money. When these people are no longer useful to them, they are discarded.

The goal of therapy with people with anti-social personalities is not to create empathetic, self-sacrificing individuals with guilt. You are unlikely to achieve this. The goal is to adapt their sociopathic behavior and help them learn that playing by the rules can actually make them look better in the long run and get them lots of rewards: it's better being a success in real estate than being kingpin of the penitentiary. The challenge for the counselor is to convince anti-social clients that it is in their best interest to change. Counselors need to position themselves as experts who can help clients stop making mistakes. Lying is an example of a mistake. Therefore, honesty is the "smart" way of relating to people.

> The three C's summarize our treatment strategies for working with clients with anti-social personalities.[3]

First you must *corral* them. Without the "walls" provided by locked doors or legal mandates, most of these clients will generally not stick around for treatment. Contingency contracts loaded with bottom line negative consequences like going to jail or losing a job are helpful. Don't get fooled by the "I got caught" moment of remorse. This is merely a brief malfunction of their defense system. It is, however, an opportune time to get a Step One started. Age can be important here. Intervention in childhood and early adolescence is often effective because the lifestyle is less entrenched, and authority figures retain more control. Adolescents are easier to corral on a secure unit where treatment staff have more control of rewards and consequences. Also peer pressure can be most helpful with anti-social adolescents. They want to maintain a good image for peers.

Older people with anti-social personalities sometimes experience a depressive crisis in their late thirties or early forties as their physiology slows down and their long-term failure to maintain themselves as "king of the mountain" sinks in. Even in these cases, external circumstances — for example, the family, or legal problems — are most often forcing the client into treatment, and may provide the only motivation to assist the client in re-evaluating his or her failing value system.

Second, you must *confront* the thinking and behavior of anti-social people. The counselor needs to help them face the mistakes in their thinking, how they think about the world, and how this thinking has not gotten them what they want. The counselor serves as a mirror showing these clients how the world and society view their behavior.

The thinking errors presented at the end of this chapter in Table Seven (pages 53-56) will give you a useful framework for confronting the process of anti-social thinking. Based on studies of the criminal personality, this list of thinking errors represents denial, projection, and rationalization broken down into finer detail.[4]

Persons with an anti-social personality disorder view the world through a distorted lens that allows them to avoid responsibility for their behavior and to maintain their "look good" image. The counselor familiar with the material in Table Seven can use these labels to comment on process and to avoid power struggles around content. Don't argue with clients about the number of legal convictions they may have. Instead, point out clients' lying by commission, omission, or assent. Do this again and again. Position yourself as helpful in relation to your clients, and not as a critical authority figure.

Chemically dependent individuals, although they may not be anti-social, demonstrate similar patterns of denial as part of the process of their disease. Thus, counselors can also use the material in Table Seven with single diagnosis chemically dependent people; they will, however, find it an invaluable tool for the "double denial" of individuals who are both chemically dependent and evidencing an anti-social personality disorder.

> **W**e have found it most helpful to begin a session with an anti-social client by developing a positive rapport.

Discuss with the client what his or her goals of counseling are, such as "staying out of jail," "getting my wife off my back," and so on. Once you have found a mutual goal, discuss how you might be helpful in assisting the client to reach this goal. Establish that the two of you will be working together to achieve goals by examining the client's thinking patterns that are at the core of his or her problem. Get the client to agree to you pointing out mistakes in his or her thinking, or thinking errors he or she makes that get in the way of achieving each particular goal. Then when the client is displaying a thinking error such as blaming, minimizing, rationalizing, or lying, you can point it out without engaging in a power struggle. If the client resists, restate the treatment contract.

If you are fortunate enough to be working in a group with these clients, establish a group norm of pointing out each others' thinking errors as helpful peer confrontation. This can be extremely powerful.

The third treatment strategy for working with clients with anti-social personalities is providing *consequences* for behavior. These consequences need to be immediate, concrete, and make use of the anti-social clients' need to look good. These individuals are not big on delay of gratification and don't care about what you think unless you can back things up with something real. Real consequences are the only thing that can impact anti-social clients. They are also "slow learners" and require repetition of consequences to convince them that it's *their behavior* and not everyone else's that is causing the problem. Use access to video games, smoking privileges, and other concrete rewards. Group contingencies (all lose privileges if a member fails to show certain behavior) are useful in enlisting other anti-social clients to apply strong peer pressure for pro-social behavior.

People with anti-social personalities are at very high risk for chemical dependency.[5] They will use any and all substances. Apart from the stimulation provided by the chemicals themselves, a lifestyle with the ups and downs of heavy chemical involvement and the money, violence, and criminal status of illegal drug trafficking can be very attractive to the excitement-driven anti-social person. Status can be achieved quickly and money made overnight. College degrees are not a prerequisite for drug dealing. Many young anti-social people, suspended from school, in conflict with the family, and bored by the thought of working at a fast-food restaurant, associate with marginal groups where drug use is the norm. In turn, chemical use adds fuel to the fire, reinforcing a distorted worldview. As they become more entrenched in the negative peer group, their attitude and behavior degenerates, causing problems with parents and school authorities. As the pressures and problems increase, young anti-social people seek relief through more drug abuse and support from negative peers. The result is a rapid downward spiral.

> **D**uring the assessment process, you must assume very little of the data given to you by anti-social clients is accurate. Honesty is not a part of their value system.

Check out everything with collateral contacts and use urine drug screens and other objective measurements. Remember, the telephone can be your friend and a constant source of data. Data is needed to develop a true picture of anti-social people's behavior. Continued vigilance of this sort must be maintained throughout treatment and aftercare if clients are to stay on track.

The Twelve Step recovery model can be very effective with these individuals when combined with the strategies outlined in this chapter. Step One is crucial and gets at a core treatment issue. We insist on *surrender* by these clients. They must understand they are not in control of either their chemical use or its consequences. The basic message is that "you are not in charge." By structuring your program and using proper techniques, the initial "I got caught" depression provides a chink in anti-social clients' defenses.

We quite often insist on at least twenty-five pages of Step One work and generally return the first draft, saying it's not good enough. It is important that the anti-social person learn to identify exactly how their drinking or other drug using behavior was out of control, how they had *lost* control over their behavior when drinking and using other drugs, and how *they* are powerless. Requiring explicit examples is helpful. We also require clients to identify the thinking errors they use to justify their chemical use and maintain their denial system. "How do you blame, manipulate, lie, and so on, to justify your use and control others?" "What are the negative consequences for you of that behavior?" is the key treatment focus.

About the Step-Work Handouts in This Chapter . . .

We then proceed with further Step work, always with an eye toward the manifestation of thinking errors. Sometimes you can also convince anti-social clients to be the very *best* recovering person in the world, chairing great AA meetings and giving talks to civic groups. Their need to "look good" can be a powerful recovery tool. They can feel *important* by helping others get sober through Twelve Step work.

Outpatient work with anti-social people is often difficult if external controls aren't in place. Outpatient providers seldom have the external control necessary to force surrender externally, and anti-social people lack the internal controls and motivation. Standard outpatient chemical dependency programs usually manage the thinking errors of chemically dependent individuals well, but in our experience, genuine anti-social people are too disruptive for most outpatient chemical dependency programs to treat successfully. They are good pretenders and act like they are following the program by day while getting high at night. Referral to a residential or inpatient dual diagnosis program with expertise in dealing with anti-social people (and the ability to restrain acting out) and with the backup provided by parental consent or court mandates is generally necessary for successful treatment.

Remember, anti-social people get clean and sober for their own reasons, not your reasons. Go for pro-recovery behavior and don't worry about motivation. It is unlikely they will develop genuine remorse and altruistic reasons for staying clean and sober. However, they may be interested if it will help them win at poker, make more money, or stay out of jail.

The following includes Table Seven, which outlines the common thinking errors of both alcoholics and anti-social people We have also included Step-work handouts on the first four Steps to be used with anti-social clients. By using this material and by maintaining our own patience and tenacity, we have been successful in helping many anti-social people obtain and maintain sobriety.

> **C**omments for facilitators regarding Step work for the client with an anti-social personality disorder appear on pages 107-108.

TABLE SEVEN

ALCOHOLIC AND ANTI-SOCIAL THINKING ERRORS

AUTHORS' NOTE: For ease of reading, the following examples refer only to alcoholics, but do describe both alcoholic and anti-social thinking errors.

1. Excuse Making

Alcoholics make excuses for anything and everything. Whenever held accountable for drinking or other drug using behavior, they often give excuses. Excuses are ways of finding reasons to justify their behavior. For example: "I drink because I'm depressed." Or, "I drink because my wife doesn't understand me."

2. Blaming

Blaming is an excuse not to solve a problem, and alcoholics use blaming to excuse their behavior and build up resentment toward someone else for "causing" whatever has happened. For example: "I couldn't do it because he got in my way." "The trouble with you is you're always looking at me in a critical way." "My wife nags me too much about my drinking." Blaming permits the build up of resentments and gets the focus off the alcoholic and puts it on others.

3. Redefining

Redefining, as shown in the following example, is shifting the focus of an issue to avoid solving a problem. *Question:* "Why did you violate your abstinence contract by drinking?" *Answer:* "I felt the language in the contract was too wordy and confusing." Alcoholics use redefining to get the focus off the subject in question. Redefining also indicates ineffective thinking, of not dealing with the problem at hand.

4. Super-Optimism

"I think; therefore, it is." Super-optimistic people decide that because they want something to be a certain way, or think it will be a certain way, it will be. This permits them to function according to what they want rather than according to the facts of the situation. For example: The alcoholic will believe that he or she can stop drinking because he or she has made the decision to stop drinking, with no treatment or AA support. Super-optimistic people also believe that they can be famous, popular, strong, movie stars, rich, and so forth simply by wishing it and never taking into account the practical steps required to achieve these goals.

5. Lying

Lying is the most commonly known characteristic of alcoholic thinking. Most alcoholics lie in different ways at different times. They use lying to confuse, distort, and take the focus off their behavior. Lying takes three forms: *commission* — making things up that are simply not true; *omission* — saying partly what is true but leaving out major sections; *assent* — making believe that one agrees with someone else, or presenting or approving others' ideas in order to look good when, in fact, the person has no intention of going along with this or does not really agree. "You could say that" is an example of subtle lying by assent.

6. Making Fools Of

Alcoholics make fools of others by agreeing to do things and not following through, by saying things they don't mean, by setting others up to fight, by inviting frustrations and letting people down, and by numerous other behaviors. By putting others down, alcoholics take the focus off their own behavior.

7. Assuming

Alcoholics spend a great deal of time assuming what others think, what others feel, what others are doing. They use this assumption in service of whatever drinking activity or behavior they decide to engage in. For example: The alcoholic assumes that other people don't like him or her. This gives the alcoholic an excuse to blow up, be angry, or get drunk. Assuming takes place every day, and alcoholics make assumptions about whatever they wish in order to support their alcoholic behavior.

8. "I'm Unique"

Alcoholics believe they are unique and special and no one else is like them. So any information that is applied to other people simply doesn't affect them. Examples of these kinds of beliefs include: "I don't need anyone, and no one understands me anyway." "No one can tell me what to do." Alcoholics in early treatment commonly believe that everyone else is alcoholic except themselves.

9. Ingratiating

Alcoholics often overdo being nice to others and going out of their way to act interested in other people. They are out to find out what they can get from other people, how they can manipulate them, use them, or control the situation for their own purpose. Watch out for praise from an alcoholic regarding your counseling skills!

10. Fragmented Personality

It is very common for alcoholics to attend church on Sunday, get drunk and in trouble on Tuesday, and then attend church again on Wednesday. To alcoholics, there is no inconsistency in this behavior. They believe they are justified in whatever they do. They see their actions as things that they deserve to do, or get, or own, or possess, or control. They never consider the inconsistency between these behaviors.

11. Minimizing

Alcoholics often minimize their behavior and actions by talking about them in such a way that they seem insignificant. They discount the significance of their behavior. You will see minimizing when confronting them about some irresponsible behavior. For example: "I only drank three beers; I could have drank a lot more, but I didn't."

12. Vagueness

Alcoholics are typically unclear and nonspecific to avoid being pinned down on any particular issue. They use words and phrases that are lacking in detail. This way they can look good to others but not commit themselves to anything specific. Examples of vague words include phrases such as: "I more or less think so." "I guess." "Probably." "Maybe." "I might." "I'm not sure about this." "It probably was." "I drink socially." "I smoke pot occasionally."

13. Anger

Anger is a primary emotion for alcoholics. This is not real anger most of the time (in fact, 99 percent of the time). Instead, alcoholics use the "anger" to control others or to use power in a situation. They have unrealistic expectations about the people in their world, and they control others by aggression, attacking, criticizing, or any other way they can to immobilize others and give themselves control of the situation.

14. Power Plays

Alcoholics use power plays whenever they aren't getting their way in a situation. This includes such things as walking out of a room during a disagreement, not completing a job they agreed to do, refusing to listen or hear what someone else has to say, or organizing people to be angry at others in their support.

15. Victim Playing

This is a major role that alcoholics take. The underlying issues are aggression and power plays. However, alcoholics act as if they are unable to solve problems or do anything for themselves. They often whine, shuffle, look woebegone and helpless, and act as if they are too stupid to do anything for themselves. Their belief is that if they don't get whatever they want, then they are victims. Victim playing elicits criticism, rescue, or enabling behavior from those around them, while it helps them avoid taking responsibility for their own behavior.

16. Drama/Excitement

Because alcoholics do not live a real life in the sense of getting their needs met directly, they often create drama and excitement. Excitement is a distraction that keeps the focus off their own behavior and drinking.

17. Closed-Minded

Alcoholics are secretive and often closed-minded. They need to protect their drinking lifestyle. Therefore, when confronted with data about their behavior, they are closed-minded and refuse to acknowledge the input, as it might jeopardize their continued drinking.

18. Image

Alcoholics' image of themselves is important to maintain. Even a late-stage, skid row alcoholic will express concern at being seen at an AA meeting.

19. Grandiosity

Grandiosity is minimizing or maximizing the significance of an issue, and it is used to justify not solving a problem. For example: "I've spilled more booze than you drank." "I can drink everyone under the table and drive them all home, so I'm not alcoholic."

20. Intellectualizing

Using academic, abstract, or theoretical discussions to avoid dealing with feelings or the real issues.

STEP ONE

"We admitted we were powerless over alcohol — that our lives had become unmanageable."

PART 1

Give five examples of ways you have tried to control your use of chemicals and failed (minimum of 100 words each).

AS

PART 2

Give five examples of people you have tried and failed to control, and explain why your controlling behavior was unsuccessful (minimum of 150 words each).

PART 3

Give five examples of situations not associated directly with drinking or using other drugs where you have tried to control things and failed (minimum of 100 words each).

(Step One, continued)

PART 4

Give two examples of people who currently have control over you, and explain how that is helpful to you (minimum of 100 words each).

(Step One, continued)

PART 5

Give ten examples of how your drinking and using other drugs caused you problems (minimum of 25 words each).

PART 6

Give five examples of negative consequences that await you should you continue using or abusing alcohol or other drugs (minimum of 50 words each).

STEP TWO

"Came to believe that a Power greater than ourselves could restore us to sanity."

PART 1

Repeating the same mistake over and over when you continually receive negative consequences is one definition of insanity. From the list below, identify *your* "mistakes" (place a check mark on the line next to each "mistake" that applies). Then, below the list, explain how each of these mistakes in your thinking has caused you problems.

_____ Excuse making

_____ Blaming

_____ Redefining

_____ Super-optimism

_____ Lying: commission, omission, assent

_____ Making fools of others

_____ Assuming what others think, feel, are doing

_____ Thinking "I'm unique"

_____ Ingratiating (kissing up)

_____ Fragmented personality — inconsistency in behavior

_____ Minimizing

_____ Intentionally being vague

_____ Using anger and threats

_____ Using power plays

_____ Playing the victim

_____ Love for drama and excitement

_____ Not listening to others — being closed minded

_____ Maintaining an "image"

_____ Being grandiose

_____ Intellectualizing

AS

PART 2

List three people you are currently angry at and explain how they can be helpful to you (minimum of 25 words each).

PART 3

List five people more powerful than you who can help you stay clean and sober. Explain why and how each person can help (minimum of 25 words each).

PART 4

Who or what is your Higher Power? (Minimum of 25 words.)

PART 5

Describe how this Higher Power can help you with your mistakes in thinking (minimum of 100 words).

STEP THREE

"Made a decision to turn our will and our lives over to the care of God as we understood Him."

PART 1

How did you decide that you needed to turn your will over to a Higher Power? (Minimum of 100 words.)

AS

PART 2

Why is it important for you to turn your will and life over to a Higher Power? (Minimum of 50 words.)

PART 3

Explain how you go about "turning it over" (minimum of 50 words).

AS

(Step Three, continued)

PART 4

Give three examples of things you have had to "turn over" in the last week (minimum of 50 words each).

AS

PART 5

Give three examples of things you have *yet* to turn over and explain how and when you plan to do so (minimum of 75 words each).

PART 6

What does it mean to "turn your will and life over to your Higher power"? (Minimum of 100 words.)

PART 7

Without displaying *any* thinking errors, explain how and why you have turned your will and life over to a Power greater than yourself (minimum of 150 words).

STEP FOUR

"Made a searching and fearless moral inventory of ourselves."

PART 1

List any and all law violations you have committed regardless of whether or not you were caught for these crimes (minimum of 100 words total).

AS

PART 2

List every person you have a resentment against, and explain how this resentment is hurting *you* (minimum of ten examples, at least 200 words total).

(Step Four, continued)

PART 3

Give ten examples of sexual behavior you engaged in that was harmful to your partner, and explain the negative consequences to *you* for this behavior (minimum of 50 words each).

PART 4

Give five examples of aggressive behavior (either verbal or physical) you
have been involved in, and explain how it was hurtful to the other person
and to *you* (minimum of 50 words each).

(Step Four, continued)

PART 5

List five major lies you have told, and explain how that lying was hurtful to *you* (minimum of 50 words each).

PART 6

List three lies you have told within the last forty-eight hours, and explain how this lying hurts your recovery program (minimum of 50 words each).

CHAPTER EIGHT

BORDERLINE PERSONALITY DISORDER

The client with a borderline personality disorder may be the greatest single challenge for the helping professional. We describe these people as "stably unstable." They experience an unstable self-image, fluctuating moods, and have chaotic, troublesome interpersonal relationships.[1] At his or her core, the borderline person is a neglected, frightened, and an abused child who is desperately seeking unconditional love. He or she operates in a world of ambivalence.

Individuals with a borderline personality disorder desperately seek the love and nurturing they never received as a child. Yet, while reaching out, they also fear that significant others will abuse and abandon them. They organize themselves around safety issues, trying to balance their approach-avoidance feelings toward others with getting their needs met in a way that feels safe. These safety operations often take the form of anti-social defenses, which attempt to combine entanglement with others with the safety provided by manipulation and acting out.[2] *Help me, help me, but you can't* is the common message of borderline clients. The counselor attempting to establish therapeutic closeness and rapport will experience a very negative response by them. They will pull back, and then, for no apparent reason, try to get close again. This on-again, off-again quality of therapy can be very frustrating for the counselor.

Borderline people are crisis-prone and polysymptomatic. Chronic depression, self-destructive behavior, and thinking with a psychotic-like edge are common problems. Eating disorders, somatic complaints, and anger outbursts are also common. Borderline individuals are prone to involvement in relationships that tend to have a hot-one-minute, cold-the-next quality and that are sometimes abusive. Quite often, the end of such a relationship triggers the crisis that brings them to treatment.

The borderline person combines characteristics of the anti-social, neurotic, and psychotic conditions. Anti-social defenses maintain the illusion of firm boundaries and power in the face of an unsafe world. The borderline person is quite often angry, manipulative, self-centered, and shows various thinking errors. But underneath this puffed-up veneer is a very frightened person who feels not only small and powerless, but also vulnerable to being engulfed by the world. As counselors, we feel pushed away by the anti-social part but remain hooked into the client because we sense the desperate, needy, and terrified part within him or her.

Both theoretical speculations and an increasing amount of research indicate that a severely dysfunctional family provokes the borderline condition. Typically, people with borderline personalities have experienced not only emotional neglect, but also intense and prolonged physical and sexual abuse.[3,4,5] One way to characterize a borderline personality is someone who has a profound and chronic kind of post-traumatic stress disorder, someone who grew up in a family "war zone."[6]

Within this framework, the goal of treatment is to help these victims become survivors. Immediately pounding on their anti-social defenses and prompting them to recall the trauma only re-victimizes these individuals. It is not the way to proceed.

> The trick is to balance building up and chipping away. We use the three S's to guide our therapeutic strategies with borderline clients.

The first objective is to provide *safety*. In times of crisis this often means inpatient treatment, with a preference for relatively short stays to avoid regression. Kind but firm limits within the frame of safety are necessary and useful for these clients who are out-of-control and view setting limits as punishment and engulfment. We use "no self-harm" contracts extensively, sometimes contracting hour by hour in inpatient settings, and week by week in outpatient settings. Negotiation also helps these people feel more in control. We help them identify and use sources of social support such as a case manager, the local crisis line, and issues groups such as AA and, if ready, incest survivors groups. We also help them pinpoint situations or events likely to trigger a self-destructive crisis, and plan and practice alternative behaviors. A matter-of-fact message of "we will help you remain safe" is the essence of these interventions. Because borderline clients will have a crisis sooner or later, we attend to these issues even if they are not currently in a crisis.

The second objective is to focus on *strengths*. Many persons with borderline personalities never learned basic self-care skills in their family of origin. The lack of good role-models and emotional support, as well as their preoccupation with the trauma they experienced, produced a developmental arrest. Focusing on clients' accomplishments also builds up positive self-regard and combats poor self-esteem. We like to work on time management skills to assist these people in structuring their day and week. Helping clients identify and use recreational outlets and develop and practice positive self-talk and affirmations are all useful activities. We especially like assertiveness training. We view this as a way to help clients use words, not acting out and self-harm, to deal with anger and to safely get their needs met.

The final objective is to do *survivor* work. Only when clients have developed ways to maintain safety and have acquired coping skills do we proceed with this type of work.[7] In survivor work we begin to address sexual or abuse issues. We start at a very intellectual level and avoid expressive, feeling-oriented approaches. We ask clients to read and attend classes about dysfunctional families and survivor issues. The intention is to help the client develop defenses, using intellectualizing and isolation (facts without feelings). Later work is more expressive and feeling-oriented and focuses on working through the trauma.

> **W**e have developed a model for the treatment of people with a borderline personality disorder that helps us understand the therapy tasks facing us and our clients.

As with individuals who have the disease of chemical dependency, those in recovery from a borderline personality disorder are never "recovered" but are always "recovering." These clients also proceed through four stages of recovery and, in fact, spiral through these stages in treatment many times. Hopefully, each re-enactment of a stage is briefer, less intense, and less frequent as these clients make progress. Each stage of recovery determines the objectives and counseling tactics most likely to benefit these clients. Table Eight on page 85 outlines these four stages and their associated indications, as well as the goals of treatment and useful therapy interventions for each stage. This model is very helpful in organizing counseling efforts in the face of these clients' typical chaotic, polysymptomatic, and crisis-prone presentation and course.

Borderline people are very prone to chemical dependency. They often come from families in which members (including the perpetrator) abused chemicals. As victims, they were sometimes given chemicals as part of the abuse scenario. They continue this cycle by abusing chemicals themselves to seek relief from the emotional pain. Borderline people often present with episodic but intense use of alcohol and other drugs. The progression seen in the classic alcoholic client may be difficult to identify in borderline clients due to their pattern of use. In our substance abuse histories on borderline clients, we've seen periods of heavy use followed by periods of apparent abstinence when they engaged in another compulsion. This compulsion centered on either food, sex, gambling, membership in a cult, or involvement in an intense romantic relationship. Borderline people use a variety of drugs, but there is almost always some use of prescription medications. Physical dependence, if there is any, most likely will be on a tranquilizer, sedating anti-depressant, or narcotic prescribed by a well-meaning but frustrated physician eager to help (or at least placate) the borderline client.

Be careful of using autobiographies when doing Fourth Step work — the telling of one's "story." This can flood these clients with unmanageable feelings as they recall their trauma. With people suffering from a severe borderline condition, we often skip the autobiography altogether and focus on more current issues.

About the Step-Work Handouts in This Chapter . . .

When using the Twelve Steps we have found certain modifications helpful. When working Step One, it is important to focus more on the unmanageability of the alcohol and other drug use than on powerlessness. The counselor should assist borderline clients in identifying situations and problems that indicate their chemical use was out of control. Go easy on the concept of powerlessness. Surrender can terrify these people. Remember, they are survivors. Focus *only* on powerlessness as it relates to alcohol and other drug use, not to other areas of their lives. Surrender can be explored later on, but only after some strengthening and building of more helpful coping skills. Premature attempts to get borderline people to surrender and admit powerlessness in Step One will be met with acting out and intensified denial.

Modifications of other Steps are also useful. Step Two — "Came to believe that a Power greater than ourselves could restore us to sanity" — is a step of faith. In non-borderline clients we attempt to expand on faith and how things are getting better now that they are abstinent.

> **B**orderline people are living life moment-to-moment. For them to have faith or hope that things will be any different is very difficult.

What we try to do is take Step Two in small pieces. We ask people to discuss how their drinking or using other drugs was insane or caused them problems. We ask them to give two examples of positive things that have happened since not using. Have them find even small instances of positive events in their lives since abstinence. We take this concept one piece at a time. The concept of a Higher Power is also extremely difficult for borderline people and requires a great deal of individualization. Do they believe in God? If so, do they believe God let them down? When exploring this subject we allow clients the freedom to say, "I feel unsafe or overwhelmed and want to stop for now." We don't push them when they are at a crisis stage. If they are having problems developing a Higher Power, we recommend Alcoholics Anonymous meetings or working the Twelve Steps. The program and the Steps can serve as their Higher Power. We discourage satanic- or cult-related higher powers, as it is our experience that they do not assist in maintaining long-term sobriety.

Step Three states, "Made a decision to turn our will and our lives over to the care of God *as we understood Him.*" We work this Step with border-line clients in the same way we would with any client. We try to assist them in learning to let go of obsessive thinking and trying to control other people, places, and things. Remember that control is central to borderline clients. They will have difficulty with this concept. Try to keep the con-cepts concrete and specific to the here and now. Focusing on their at-tempts to control through drama and excitement is useful for clients who defend by creating chaos.

We prefer that the borderline client complete Steps Four and Five in a safe inpatient or residential setting unless the client has shown some stability for at least six months. Otherwise, regressions can occur.

Step Four states, "Made a searching and fearless moral inventory of ourselves." This can be an extremely volatile Step for borderline people. We have modified this Step in the following ways: (1) we have clients start their inventory from age twelve and up, and (2) we require clients to list an equal amount of positives or strengths as well as "character defects."

We encourage AA or NA attendance. Borderline people can benefit from the support these meetings provide. We tell our borderline clients that they might not like a particular meeting, and we encourage them to be in control of which meeting they prefer to attend. We discourage attendance at ACOA (Adult Children of Alcoholics) meetings until later in their recovery. The emphasis on feeling work and relative lack of struc-ture often found at these meetings, while useful for the non-borderline adult child of an alcoholic, is not good for the borderline client. It can lead to relapse into alcohol or other drugs as well as self-destructive behavior. We also recommend a same-sex sponsor. Due to the poor sexual bound-aries and dependency needs many of these clients demonstrate, unfortu-nate relationships can develop that prove destructive to both the sponsor and the client.

Borderline people, as part of their survivor skills, are exquisitely sensi-tive to other people's "buttons" and will skillfully push them. Counselors who are vulnerable to enabling and rescuing, who insist clients must get well or be considered bad, who have weak boundaries themselves, or who rely heavily on self-disclosure, are not ideal for working with borderline clients. The key for managing a counseling relationship with borderline clients is a matter-of-fact, here-and-now attitude. The AA slogans — first things first, one day at a time — are most helpful. We also hope for the best, expect the worst, and settle for what we can get when working with borderline clients.

Specialized Step-work handouts on the first four Steps designed for borderline clients follow Table Eight.

Comments for facilitators regarding Step work for the borderline client appear on pages 109-110.

TABLE EIGHT
RECOVERY MODEL FOR THE TREATMENT OF BORDERLINE PERSONALITY DISORDER

Stage	Indications	Goal	Interventions
I. Crisis	behavior out of control; risk of harm to self or others; extreme withdrawal or intrusiveness	safety and health through structure and support	• inpatient stay • contracts for safety • case manager or support groups • identify triggers for relapse or stress to plan for crisis • daily or weekly schedule to structure time
II. Building	routine attendance at therapeutic sessions, meetings, appointments; some ability to stay focused on here and now	increasing coping skills and self-esteem	• develop an assets or accomplishments list • positive self-talk and affirmations • skills training in time management, assertiveness, and so on
III. Education	expresses, exhibits increased self-efficacy	reframe self and history from victim to survivor	• read or debrief ACOA or incest-survivor literature • classes on dysfunctional families, survivor issues • written assignments on strengths and limitations of "survivor" behaviors
IV. Integrations	able to express feelings, regulate thinking and actions	integrate past, present, and current feelings, thoughts, behaviors	• art therapy, journal work, other expressive modalities • psychodynamic therapy, here-and-now interpretations • grief and child-within work, marital, sex, or family therapy

STEP ONE

"We admitted we were powerless over alcohol — that our lives had become unmanageable."

PART 1

Describe five situations where you suffered negative consequences as a result of drinking or using other drugs.

BL

PART 2

List at least five "rules" you have about drinking or using other drugs that you developed in order to try to control your drinking or your use of other drugs. (Example: "I never drink alone.")

PART 3

Tell where and how you broke each rule discussed in Part 2. Give one example for each rule.

BL

PART 4

Check the following that apply to you.

_____ I sometimes drink or use other drugs more than I plan.

_____ I sometimes lie about my drinking or use of other drugs.

_____ I have hidden or stashed away alcohol or other drugs
so I could use them alone or at a later time.

_____ I have had memory loss when drinking or using other drugs.

_____ I have tried to hurt myself when drinking or using other drugs.

_____ I can drink or use more than I used to, without feeling drunk or high.

_____ My personality changes when I drink or use other drugs.

_____ I have school or work problems related to my drinking or use of
other drugs.

_____ I have family problems related to my drinking or use of other
drugs.

_____ I have legal problems related to my drinking or use of other drugs.

PART 5

Give two examples for each item checked in Part 4.

STEP TWO

"Came to believe that a Power greater than ourselves could restore us to sanity."

PART 1

Give three examples of how your drinking or use of other drugs was insane. (Remember, one definition of *insanity* is to keep repeating the same mistake and expecting a different outcome.)

BL

PART 2

Check which of the mistakes or thinking errors you use.

_____ Blaming
_____ Lying
_____ Manipulating
_____ Excuse making
_____ Minimizing
_____ Beating yourself up with "I should have"
_____ Self-mutilation (cutting on self when angry)
_____ Negative self-talk
_____ Intellectualizing
_____ Using angry behavior to control others
_____ Thinking *I'm Unique*

Explain below how each thinking error you checked above is harmful to you and others.

(Step Two, continued)

PART 3

Give two examples of something that has happened since you stopped drinking or using other drugs that shows you how your situation is improving.

PART 4

Who or what is your Higher Power?

Why do you think your Higher Power can be helpful to you?

STEP THREE

"Made a decision to turn our will and our lives over to the care of God as we understood Him."

PART 1

Explain how and why you decided to turn your will over to a Higher Power.

PART 2

Give two examples of things or situations you have turned over in the last week.

(Step Three, continued)

PART 3

List two current resentments you have, and explain why it is important for you to turn them over to your Higher Power.

PART 4

How do you go about "turning over a resentment"?

(Step Three, continued)

PART 5

What does it mean to turn your will and life over to your Higher Power?

PART 6

Explain how and why you have turned your will and life over to a Power greater than yourself.

BL

STEP FOUR

"Made a searching and fearless moral inventory of ourselves."

PART 1

List five things you like about yourself.

PART 2

Give five examples of situations where you have been helpful to others.

BL

PART 3

Give three examples of sexual behaviors related to your drinking or use of other drugs, which have occurred in the last five years, that you feel badly about.

PART 4

Describe how beating yourself up for old drinking and other drug using behavior is *not* helpful to your recovery.

BL

PART 5

List five current resentments you have, and explain how holding on to these resentments hurts your recovery.

PART 6

List all laws you have broken related to your drinking and use of other drugs.

(Step Four, continued)

PART 7

List three new behaviors you have learned that are helpful to your recovery.

PART 8

List all current fears you are experiencing, and discuss how working the first three Steps can help dissolve them.

PART 9

Give an example of a current situation you are handling poorly.

PART 10

Discuss how you plan to handle the situation you described in Part 9 differently the next time the situation arises.

BL

SUMMARY

Dually diagnosed clients need simultaneous treatment for coexisting disorders. Integrating Twelve Step and mental health approaches has, in our experience, helped many "untreatable" clients begin their recovery from *both* chemical dependency *and* their psychiatric disorder.

The following is a summary of general treatment tips discussed at greater length in this workbook. Readers interested in a more comprehensive overview of the treatment of dually diagnosed clients will benefit from reading our book *Dual Diagnosis: Counseling the Mentally Ill Substance Abuser*. Readers will find specific guidelines for specialized Step work in the Comments for Facilitators section on page 105 of this workbook.

Treatment Tips for Dually Diagnosed Clients with the Most Common Major Mental and Emotional Disorders

Schizophrenia

1. Emphasize medication compliance; make a distinction between good drugs and bad drugs. Watch for anti-cholenergic medication abuse.
2. Keep it simple and concrete; use visual learning materials; repeat often with attention-getting style; practice specific situations. Use flash cards, checklists, frequent feedback. Think *structure*.
3. Emphasize unmanageability, three reasons to stay clean and sober, and three reasons to take medication. Be satisfied with a good Step One.
4. Be careful of Higher Power concept; refocus onto a person or thing that could help; focus on how things are a little better.
5. Provide housing, case manager, day treatment with attention to chemical use issues.
6. Find or start sympathetic AA groups. Formulate plan with client and sponsor to handle challenge of medication use.

Bipolar Disorder (Manic-Depression)

1. Avoid thinking that chemical use is secondary to mood swings.
2. Use lithium and distinguish between medication and chemicals. Emphasize medication compliance.
3. Channel energy by setting limits, giving permission for limited hypomania. Keep assignments short, stay concrete, and keep structure in individual and group sessions.

4. Avoid challenging grandiose notions, limit Higher Power issues, and stay concrete.
   5. Help client and sponsor to structure interactions.

Major Depression
   1. Distinguish if client is suffering from organic affective disorder or adjustment reaction (grief) due to chemical use, or if it is true major depression. Distinguish whether it's an endogenous or a character-based depression. Don't be too quick to relieve the grief of chemically dependent person.
   2. Use medication conservatively and only if endogenous symptoms persist. Plan for the client being challenged in self-help groups because of medication use.
   3. Facilitate grief work as part of Step work. Emphasize powerlessness in Step One; faith and hope in Steps Two and Three.
   4. Build a social support system, push for increased behavior rate, and gently challenge depressive cognitions. Use AA attendance, a sponsor, and Step work to help with this.

Anxiety Disorders
   1. Watch for benzodiazepine and alcohol abuse.
   2. Inform clients that prescription medication is also a chemical and that they must take responsibility for informing physicians of their chemical dependency.
   3. Consider an evaluation for use of anti-depressants for panic attacks and obsessive-compulsive disorders.
   4. Use behavioral methods (relaxation, graded exposure, and response prevention) for all anxiety disorders.
   5. Use Step work to deal with control issues.
   6. Watch for codependency issues, either as cause or effect.

Organic Mental Disorders
   1. Recovery from chronic conditions is minimal after one year and requires abstinence from chemicals.
   2. Assess strengths and limitations with neuropsychological tests and design an individual approach.
   3. Watch for "talks good — can't do" problems.
   4. Emphasize strongly that a damaged brain doesn't need chemicals.
   5. Aim for a good Step One, but be realistic.
   6. Use teaching techniques that help clients with schizophrenic disorders.
   7. Watch for abuse of anti-seizure medication.

Treatment Tips for Dually Diagnosed Clients With the Most Common Personality Disorders

Passive-Aggressive Personality Disorder
1. Watch for prescription medication and alcohol or sedative-hypnotic abuse.
2. Hold client responsible for chemical dependency work.
3. Use ally-aware and assert approach.
4. Watch for interpersonal dependency issues.
5. Use AA and a sponsor to meet a client's need for belonging.
6. Use Step work for control issues.

Anti-Social Personality Disorder
1. Watch for polysubstance abuse and dependence. High risk for chemical dependency.
2. Use corral, confront, and consequence approach.
3. Emphasize surrender and *their* reasons for sobriety.
4. Make use of "look good" channel. Encourage them to be the best recovering person in the world.
5. Assess family and look for signs of codependency.

Borderline Personality Disorder
1. Watch for episodic polysubstance abuse.
2. Use safety, strengths, survivor approach.
3. Emphasize unmanageability in Step One, current improvements and others who could be helpful in Step Two. Be careful of autobiography in Step Four and possibly dredging up childhood trauma before client is ready to deal with this.
4. Avoid enabling and keep clear boundaries. Maintain here-and-now, matter-of-fact attitude.

We have found working with the dually diagnosed client to be both challenging and rewarding. We hope this workbook has proven to be a helpful addition to your therapeutic repertoire.

COMMENTS FOR FACILITATORS

STEP WORK FOR THE CLIENT WITH SCHIZOPHRENIA OR AN ORGANIC MENTAL DISORDER

Step 1

Key concepts:
- Focus on concrete, basic examples. Remember keep it simple
- Emphasize specific examples of unmanageable behavior
- Ask clients to develop cue cards to learn concepts — for example, assist them in writing on one card "three reasons I can't drink or use," and, on the other card, "three reasons I should take my medication"

Watch out for the following:
- Abstract discussions of powerlessness
- Paranoid thinking
- Cryptic, weird, unusual responses
- Vague, rambling responses

Step 2

Key concepts:
- Goal is to teach faith and hope
- Use concrete examples of how things are better today than yesterday since stopping chemicals and starting medication
- Instead of God or Higher Power, ask for a concrete example of a *person* who is helpful
- Role-play, asking for help

Watch out for the following:
- Lengthy discussions of God or Higher Power
- Discussions of "Evil" or the "Devil"
- Loose, rambling responses
- Denial that anyone could be helpful

Step 3

Key concepts:

- Keep examples in the here-and-now and be specific
- List helpful people — for example, case managers, doctors
- Insist on current examples of worries
- Role-play, discussing this worry with helpful person

Watch out for the following:

- Discussions of God, Jesus, or Higher Power. Avoid girlfriends or drinking buddies as helpful people
- Denial of worry or anxiety
- Loose, rambling content

STEP WORK FOR THE CLIENT WITH A BIPOLAR DISORDER (MANIC DEPRESSION)

Step 1

Key concepts:

- Keep responses brief and specific
- Set maximum word lengths
- No abstract discussion
- Focus on specific examples of unmanageability
- Brief discussion of out-of-control behavior from both mania and addiction are helpful

Watch out for the following:

- Abstract discussion of Higher Power or God
- Grandiose ideas that *they alone* are the answer to their problems
- Ideas that they are unique and can manage without the Twelve Steps and self-help groups
- Rambling, vague ideas for "great" plans for improving the world
- Philosophical discussions of powerlessness

Step 2

Key concepts:
- Discuss thinking errors
- Keep examples specific, brief, and clear
- Discuss unmanageability of mania as well as abuse of alcohol and other drugs
- Emphasize faith and hope — specific examples of how things are better today than yesterday since stopping chemicals and starting medication

Watch out for the following:
- Loose, grandiose discussions
- Minimizing problems or need for alternative behavior
- Intellectualizing

Step 3

Key concepts:
- Keep examples specific, brief, and clear
- Identify a *person* that can be helpful
- Role-play, asking for help

Watch out for the following:
- Intellectual discussions of *if* there is a God or *who* God is
- Belief that they need help from no one
- Unusual or bizarre ideas of Higher Power

STEP WORK FOR THE ANTI-SOCIAL CLIENT

Step 1

Key concepts:
- Emphasize surrender
- Support "their" reason for being sober (to stay out of jail, etcetera)
- Require *minimums* of 50 to 100 words (simply completing the Step-work handouts is a type of surrender!)
- Specific examples of problems related to drinking and using as well as "mistakes" in thinking
- Strive for and reinforce honesty
- Hold person accountable

Watch out for the following:
- The use of thinking errors (blaming, rationalizing, etcetera)
- Sloppy or minimum efforts which do not meet requirements
- Lost Step work

Step 2

Key concepts:
- Continue to require word minimums
- Ensure client recognized "mistakes" in their thinking
- Examples should be specific and complete and include all criminal behaviors committed, not just the ones convicted of

Watch out for the following:
- Thinking errors (particularly blaming, minimizing, and justifying)
- Superficial or incomplete work

Step 3

Key concepts:
- Support idea that they need help to meet *their* goal (stay out of jail, etcetera)
- Reinforce how asking for help is "cool"
- Point out how resentments hurt only themselves *not* the ones they are angry at
- Role-play, asking for help

Watch out for the following:
- Ridiculous Higher Power, such as trees, doorknobs, or toilet seats
- Unrealistic plans for how to get help

Step 4

Key concepts:
- Reinforce honesty and thoroughness
- Keep examples specific to how they acted poorly, not how *someone else* acted poorly
- Point out *their* responsibility in the problem and the solution

Watch out for the following:
- Sarcasm
- Superficial, glossed-over work
- Thinking errors
- Excuses on why Step Four isn't necessary

STEP WORK FOR THE BORDERLINE CLIENT

Step 1

Key concepts:
- Focus on unmanageability or drinking and using behavior
- Keep examples specific to drinking and using drugs

Watch out for the following:
- Negative global thinking (*Nothing can help me*)
- Discussions of powerlessness or helplessness

Step 2

Key concepts:
- Limit insanity discussions to only drinking and using other drugs
- Identify thinking errors related to drinking and using as well as other unmanageable behavior
- Emphasize small, specific signs of progress

Watch out for the following:
- Vague or unclear statements
- Hopelessness
- Thinking errors (including victim stance)
- Preoccupation with death and dying

Step 3

Key concepts:
- Higher Power should be someone or something that can be *helpful* to sobriety — not Satan, crystals, doorknobs, or a dog
- Help emphasize that *letting go* of resentment *gives* a person *more power* to feel better
- Practice role-playing, asking for help

Watch out for the following:
- Dark, bizarre thinking — (*I'm going to die, so this isn't going to help*)
- Self-abuse
- Thinking errors

Step 4

Key concepts:

- List assets and accomplishments *before* negative traits
- Emphasize strengths
- Emphasize "sick" or "bad" behavior as part of the "disease of addiction"
- Keep focused on current resentments

Watch out for the following:

- Prematurely asking questions about early childhood trauma
- Sexual inventories
- Inability to set long-term goals
- Blaming oneself excessively

ENDNOTES

Chapter One: Schizophrenia

1.   F. R. Schneier and S. G. Siris, "Review of Psychoactive Substance Use and Abuse in Schizophrenia," *Journal of Nervous and Mental Disease* 175:11 (1987): 641-52.

Chapter Two: Bipolar Disorder (Manic-Depression)

1.   T. W. Estroff, et al., "Drug Abuse and Bipolar Disorder," *International Journal of Psychiatric Medicine* 15 (1985): 37-40.

Chapter Three: Major Depression

1.   M. R. Liepman, et al., "Depression Associated with Substance Abuse," *Presentations of Depression*, ed. O.G. Cameron (New York: John Wiley & Sons, 1987).
2.   M. N. Hesselbrock, R. E. Meyer, and J. J. Keener, "Psychopathology in Hospitalized Alcoholics," *Archives of General Psychiatry* 42 (1985): 1050-55.
3.   American Psychiatric Association, *Diagnostic and Statistical Manual of Mental Disorders*, 3rd ed., revised (Washington, D.C.: American Psychiatric Association, 1987).

Chapter Four: Anxiety Disorders

1.   American Psychiatric Association, *Diagnostic and Statistical Manual of Mental Disorders*.
2.   F. M Quitkin and J. G. Rabbin, "Hidden Psychiatric Diagnoses in the Alcoholic," *Alcoholism and Clinical Psychiatry*, ed. J. Soloman (New York: Plenum Press, 1982): 129-39.
3.   H. R. Kranzler and N. R. Liebowitz, "Anxiety and Depression in Substance Abuse," *Medical Clinics of North America* 72:4 (1988): 867-85.
4.   Quitkin and Rabbin, "Hidden Psychiatric Diagnoses in the Alcoholic."
5.   Kranzler and Liebowitz, "Anxiety and Depression in Substance Abuse."

Chapter Five: Organic Mental Disorders

1.   H. S. Peyser, "Alcoholism and Clinical Psychiatry," in *Alcoholism: A Practical Treatment Guide.* eds. S. E. Gitlow and H. S. Peyser (Philadelphia: Grune & Stratton, 1988).
2.   S. Dilsauer, "The Patho-Physiologies of Substance Abuse and Affective Disorders: An Integrative Model," *Journal of Clinical Psycho-pharmacology* 1 (1987):1-10.

3.   T. S. Tsuang, J. C. Simpson, and Z. Kronfol, "Subtypes of Drug Abuse with Psychosis," *Archives of General Psychiatry* 39 (1982): 141-147.
4.   I. Grant and R. Reed, "Neuropsychology of Alcohol and Drug Abuse," *Substance Abuse and Psychopathology*, ed. A. Alterman (New York: Plenum Press, 1985).

Chapter Six: Passive-Aggressive Personality Disorder
1.   American Psychiatric Association, *Diagnostic and Statistical Manual of Mental Disorders.*

Chapter Seven: Anti-Social Personality Disorder
1.   American Psychiatric Association, *Diagnostic and Statistical Manual of Mental Disorders.*
2.   M. A. Shuckit, "The Clinical Implications of Primary Diagnostic Groups Among Alcoholics," *Archives of General Psychiatry* 42 (1985): 1043-49.
3.   R. R. Rada, "Sociopathy and Alcoholism: Diagnostic and Treatment Implications," in *The Treatment of Antisocial Syndromes*, ed. W. H. Reid (New York: Van Nostrand and Rheinhold, 1980).
4.   S. Samenow, *Inside the Criminal Mind* (New York: Times Books/ Random House, 1984).
5.   M. D. Schukit, "Genetic and Clinical Implications of Alcoholism and Affective Disorder," *American Journal of Psychiatry* 143 (1986): 140-47.

Chapter Eight: Borderline Personality Disorder
1.   American Psychiatric Association, *Diagnostic and Statistical Manual of Mental Disorders.*
2.   J. C. Perry, "Depression in Borderline Personality Disorder: Lifetime Prevalence at Interview and Longitudinal Course of Symptoms," *American Journal of Psychiatry* 142:1 (1985): 15-21.
3.   J. B. Buyer, et. al., "Childhood Sexual Abuse and Physical Abuse as Factors in Adult Psychiatric Illness," *American Journal of Psychiatry* 144 (1987): 1426-30.
4.   A. F. Gartner and J. Gartner, "Borderline Pathology in Post-Incest Female Adolescents," *The Menninger Bulletin* 52 (1988): 101-13.
5.   M. C. Zanarini and J. B. Gunderson, "Childhood Abuse Common in Borderline Personality," *Clinical Psychiatry News* 6 (1987): 1-2.
6.   F. H. Lundberg and L. J. Distad, "Post-Traumatic Stress Disorders in Women Who Experienced Childhood Incest," *Child Abuse and Neglect* 9 (1985): 329-34.
7.   C. Bass and L. Davis, *The Courage to Heal* (New York: Harper & Row, 1988).

THE TWELVE STEPS
OF ALCOHOLICS ANONYMOUS*

1. We admitted we were powerless over alcohol — that our lives had become unmanageable.

2. Came to believe that a Power greater than ourselves could restore us to sanity.

3. Made a decision to turn our will and our lives over to the care of God *as we understood Him*.

4. Made a searching and fearless moral inventory of ourselves.

5. Admitted to God, to ourselves, and to another human being the exact nature of our wrongs.

6. Were entirely ready to have God remove all these defects of character.

7. Humbly asked Him to remove our shortcomings.

8. Made of list of all persons we had harmed, and became willing to make amends to them all.

9. Made direct amends to such people wherever possible, except when to do so would injure them or others.

10. Continued to take personal inventory and when we were wrong promptly admitted it.

11. Sought through prayer and meditation to improve our conscious contact with God *as we understood Him*, praying only for knowledge of His will for us and the power to carry that out.

12. Having had a spiritual awakening as the result of these steps, we tried to carry this message to alcoholics, and to practice these principles in all our affairs.

---

* The Twelve Steps of A.A. are taken from *Alcoholics Anonymous*, 3rd ed., published by A.A. World Services, Inc., New York, N.Y., 59-60. Reprinted with permission of A.A. World Services, Inc.

Other titles that will interest you. . .

Dual Disorders
Counseling Clients with Chemical Dependency and Mental Illness
> *by Dennis C. Daley, M.S.W.,*
> *Howard Moss, M.D., and Frances Campbell, M.S.N.*
> This primary resource book addresses the needs and concerns of patients

diagnosed as both chemically dependent and mentally ill. It discusses the most common psychiatric disorders found in conjunction with alcoholism, enabling counselors to better use assessment and counseling skills. 148 pp.
Order No. 5023

The New Drugs
Look-Alikes, Drugs of Deception, and Designer Drugs
> *by Richard Seymour, M.A., David Smith, M.D.,*
> *Darryl Inaba, Pharm. D., and Mim Landry*
> This book describes basic categories of psychoactive, abused drugs. After discuss-

ing how new drugs develop from legitimate research and home laboratory experimentation, this book provides professionals with basic identification and treatment techniques. 160 pp.
Order No. 5054

Coping with Dual Disorders
Chemical Dependency and Mental Illness
> *by Dennis Daley and Frances Campbell*
> Simply written, this large-format pamphlet offers the dual diagnosed patient help

in understanding how mental illnesses interact with and complicate chemical dependency. Activities are suggested to help the patient clearly understand the issues. 23 pp.
Order No. 5218

For price and order information please call one of our Telephone Representatives. Ask for a free catalog describing nearly 1,500 items available through Hazelden Educational Materials.

HAZELDEN EDUCATIONAL MATERIALS

1-800-328-9000	1-800-257-0070	1-612-257-4010	1-612-257-2195
(Toll Free. U.S. Only)	(Toll Free. MN Only)	(AK and Outside U.S.)	(FAX)

Pleasant Valley Road • P.O. Box 176• Center City, MN 55012-0176